MANTRAS
MADE EASY

MANTRAS *for*
HAPPINESS
PEACE
PROSPERITY
and more

SHERIANNA BOYLE, MED, CAGS

adamsmedia
avon, massachusetts

Copyright © 2017 by F+W Media, Inc.
All rights reserved.
This book, or parts thereof, may not be reproduced in any form without permission from the publisher; exceptions are made for brief excerpts used in published reviews.

Published by
Adams Media, a division of F+W Media, Inc.
57 Littlefield Street, Avon, MA 02322. U.S.A.
www.adamsmedia.com

ISBN 10: 1-4405-9997-1
ISBN 13: 978-1-4405-9997-2
eISBN 10: 1-4405-9998-X
eISBN 13: 978-1-4405-9998-9

Printed in the United States of America.

10 9 8 7 6 5 4 3 2 1

Library of Congress Cataloging-in-Publication Data

Boyle, Sherianna, author.
Mantras made easy / Sherianna Boyle, MEd, CAGS.
Avon, Massachusetts: Adams Media, 2017.
Includes index.
LCCN 2016034477 | ISBN 9781440599972 (pb) | ISBN 1440599971 (pb) | ISBN 9781440599989 (ebook) | ISBN 144059998X (ebook)
LCSH: Mantras.
LCC BL1236.22 .B65 2016 | DDC 203/.7--dc23
LC record available at https://lccn.loc.gov/2016034477

Many of the designations used by manufacturers and sellers to distinguish their products are claimed as trademarks. Where those designations appear in this book and F+W Media, Inc. was aware of a trademark claim, the designations have been printed with initial capital letters.

Cover design by Colleen Cunningham.
Cover image © Marina Kleper/123RF.

This book is available at quantity discounts for bulk purchases.
For information, please call 1-800-289-0963.

DEDICATION

Deep inside your heart is a sacred altar. Go there
now and I will meet you. Together we will recite these
words, sounds, and phrases in the name of love.

—Sherianna

This book is dedicated to the great Thomas Ashley-Farrand,
who brought many of these sacred mantras to the West, and
to all my spiritual teachers—those whom I have met, as well as
those whom I have not. You know who you are. Thank you. To
Karen Cooper and Laura Daly for your unconditional support
and belief in this project. To my daughters, Megan, Mikayla, and
Makenzie, I pass the gift of mantras to you with much love. To
my mother, for showing up to my yoga classes, and to my dear
dad. Finally, this is for you—you the reader, you the soul. Know
that these offerings go beyond me. Your interest in this book is
no accident and neither is our connection.

CONTENTS

INTRODUCTION

"A mantra truly is a vehicle that takes you into
quieter, more peaceful levels of the mind."

Deepak Chopra

Mantras are words, syllables, or phrases you repeat to help you connect and feel the energy within you and around you. Mantras can provide you with all kinds of support when you need it most—comfort, inspiration, reassurance, motivation, a sense of calm, or a burst of energy—and they can be practiced anytime, anywhere. The words in mantras are carefully formulated to offer you a way to be present and move through a particular situation. Incorporating mantras into your daily life will help you be more focused and centered, and better able to transform perceived obstacles into doorways of opportunity.

I realized this firsthand when I received a letter from my credit card company. The message informed me that personal information had been stolen by an intruder who had hacked into the computer of a company that I was ordering products from. Rather than saying, *You've gotta be kidding me!* or *Ugh!*

Such a hassle!, my mind immediately thought, *All is well*. My daily mantra practice interceded in what could have been a very stressful moment and offered me just the words I needed to think. Although I was sure to follow the necessary logistical precautions about my identity and finances, the mantra gave me the means to access a sense of calm, clarity, and resilience.

In the past, I might have panicked, analyzed the "what ifs," felt sorry for myself, or held my breath through the process. This is no longer the case. The practice of mantras not only loosens the grip of old, ineffective habits but also generously clears away what contributes to them in the first place. As a result, you free yourself of defensive coping mechanisms that previously zapped your energy, and instead you activate more liberating states of being. When this occurs, your life tends to run more smoothly, filling you with ease—less like a yo-yo (or in some cases a freight train).

When practiced and applied effectively, mantras also give you the power to positively influence others through the personal transformation of yourself. *Mantras Made Easy* is a collection of mantras for all the ups and downs of daily living. Think of it as a trusted friend, offering you just what you need to get through the particular situation you're experiencing. You'll find mantras to bring you happiness, peace, love, and healing, and mantras to help you overcome fear and anxiety. In addition to the mantras, you'll also find specific insight into why these specific words will help in the given situation.

Leave frustration, anger, and fear behind. Embrace the peace, inspiration, and happiness that mantras can provide.

1

THE POWER
OF A MANTRA

"We don't necessarily
see things as *they* are.
We see them as *we* are."

Ram Dass with Rameshwar Das,
Polishing the Mirror

According to German authors Grazyna Fosar and Franz Bludorf, your body is "programmable by language, words, and thought." Just like you are programmed to respond to the ring of your phone, you can program repeated words and phrases into your subconscious mind. If you repeat negative words and phrases, you begin to develop beliefs (e.g., I'm fat) and behaviors (acting guilty and irritable) that do not serve you well.

If that's the case for you, take heart. These tendencies are actually a reflection of our evolution. In order to survive, our ancestors were wired to focus on the negative, as this increased their chances of survival. They had to be on the lookout for predators and constantly be aware of threats to their food and water sources. Today, of course, we don't need to watch out for lions or remember how to get to a watering hole. But this information about how our brains work provides insight into why mantras are so powerful. Although focusing on the negative helped our ancestors survive, focusing on the positive through mantras is much more beneficial for the modern you.

The History of Mantras

Mantras are one of the most ancient mind-body practices. Although mantras have been around for 3,000-plus years, they were not fully discovered until the last 150 years. This is because a good portion of mantras were written in the ancient Hindu language of Sanskrit and kept private to preserve their quality. Although Sanskrit is not spoken today, it is very much kept alive through the practice of mantras.

MANTRAS IN THE BIBLE

Mantras are also found throughout the Bible. Syllables and words taken from prayers can easily be put into practice within a mantra. For example, the word *amen*, which was originally a Hebrew (Aramaic) term and made its way into Greek, Latin, and then finally English, is translated as "and so be it." Moreover, Bible passages such as "In the beginning was the Word, and the Word was with God, and the Word was God" (John 1:1) show just how important words are to the practice of faith.

Sanskrit Mantras

Thomas Ashley-Farrand, one of the western experts on sacred Sanskrit mantras, reports that mantras were originally recorded on palm leaves. Certain families were asked to safeguard specific mantras, similar to a family heirloom or a secret recipe. Mantras in India and Tibet were secured through precise recording, storing, and passing from generation to generation. All of this information was eventually transferred and formally recorded in one of the oldest Hindu texts (still widely utilized today) called the Veda.

Sanskrit mantras were designed as a tool for healing and spiritual growth. They were used to increase abundance, prosperity, strength, protection, fortitude, and love. For example, one might commit to a mantra to increase the abundance of crops, ward off diseases, and/or attract good luck.

Thousands of mantras have been recorded throughout history and many are being created in our own native language today. What makes the Sanskrit ones so special is the amazing foundation they have been built upon. You can think of Sanskrit mantras as being similar to an eternal flame. When you recite a Sanskrit mantra, you are not only tapping into the energy of the words but also the level of consciousness that was put into the words by those who repeated it before you. Since this level of consciousness goes back thousands of years, you can imagine how strong this word energy is.

Ashley-Farrand discusses how each of the Sanskrit mantras appears tailor-made to support the human energetic system. Each letter in the Sanskrit language corresponds to a chakra (energy center in the body). Making Sanskrit sounds involves your tongue tapping the roof of your mouth. This action stimulates the hypothalamus of the brain, where emotional memories are stored. It is quite remarkable how our ancestors were able to tap into this knowledge without having the scientific equipment and resources we have today.

One of the reasons Sanskrit mantras are so effective is that they use seed sounds (explained next) to connect to invisible energy centers of the body, called chakras. *Chakra* means (spinning) wheel. There are seven major chakras and many more minor ones, and they correspond to places where energy pools in the energy field of the human body. Each chakra corresponds to a specific gland, organ, or muscle, beginning at the base of the spine and continuing all the way to the top of your head. When your chakras are in balance, this creates an internal state of flow.

Chakras are often represented through images of the lotus flower. These images illustrate that each chakra has a certain amount of petals. For example, the root chakra, which is located in the pelvic floor, has been reported to have four petals. If you add up all the petals, from the base of the pelvic floor to the brow point (third eye), you get fifty-two petals all together. Ashley-Farrand points out that there is a total of fifty petals and there are also exactly fifty letters in the Sanskrit language.

Today, many spiritual leaders, priests, monks, mentors, therapists, and yogis tap into mantras as a way to live and spread the principles of love and compassion their teachers gave them.

> What makes one slogan more impactful than another? The energy it carries. Mantras, when written properly, practiced, and understood, are one of the most cherished free resources to humankind.

Believe it or not, mantras are also common in our everyday language. What started out as a catch phrase for a marketing strategy (such as Nike's "Just do it" trademark) can, with awareness, evolve into a daily mantra.

SEED SOUNDS

Sanskrit mantras are based on what are referred to as seed sounds. Seed sounds are syllables put together to create a vibration in a certain area of the body. One of the most well-known seed sounds is Om (pronounced Aum), which is often chanted before or after a yoga class. According to Swami Adiswarananda, Om "is considered the seed mantra, for it is the source of all other mantras and of all compounded sounds." Om is often used as a prefix to a mantra or an ending to a mantra. The sound of Om, when chanted regularly, balances your brain waves. According to the book *Healing Mantras* by Thomas Ashley-Farrand, Om connects you to your sixth chakra; it is "the sound heard when the masculine and feminine currents . . . meet and merge" at the brow area.

The following table notes the sounds associated with each chakra.

Chakra No.	Chakra	Location	Seed Sound
7	crown	top of head	silence after OM
6	third eye	forehead	OM
5	throat	throat	HAM
4	heart	upper chest	YAM
3	solar plexus	mid-torso	RAM
2	sacral	2 inches below navel	VAM
1	root	base of spine	LAM

GODS AND GODDESSES

Sanskrit mantras are also connected to Buddhism and the Hindu culture. Many of the mantras are believed to support an everyday person's connection to Hindu gods and goddesses such as Krishna, Shiva, and Lord Vishnu. These gods and goddesses have a wealth of wisdom and insight that, when tuned in to, can support the evolution of your spiritual development, even if you are not Buddhist. For example, Buddhist teachings are rich with insight on the value of cultivating compassion. Keep in mind when you are reciting mantras that you are not just stating the words, but also you are allowing the energy within them to transpire within you. Many of these gods and goddesses are mentioned in spiritual music, which is becoming more widespread in the West.

> Please know that choosing to incorporate Sanskrit mantras into your daily life does not mean you are changing your religion. Regardless of what religion you were raised in or practice today, you can turn to mantras and use them as tools to support the development of your meditation skills.

SANSKRIT MANTRAS TODAY

Today, Sanskrit mantras are catching the attention of neuroscientists and other mind-body researchers. Many researchers are studying the effects of a positive mindset on overall health and well-being, and mantras can certainly help facilitate a positive outlook.

Researchers such as Thomas Ashley-Farrand have dedicated their lives to preserving the roots of Sanskrit mantras, making them accessible to new generations while encouraging seekers to respect their sacred history.

How Mantras and Affirmations Are Different

Author Louise Hay is one of the pioneers of affirmations. She brings their power to light in her book *You Can Heal Your Life*. Although mantras and affirmations share a similar intention of transformation and empowerment, to effectively practice mantras it is helpful to know what distinguishes one from the other. The following table shows the differences between the two practices.

Mantras	Affirmations
Are at least 3,000 years old	Surfaced in the 1980s
Founded in spirituality	Founded in psychology
Energy-focused	Statement-focused
Can be as short as a single syllable	Are usually a full sentence
Are repeated more frequently	Are repeated less often

Mantras and affirmations both have a place in meditative study. Mantras' long history and connection to energy influence the development of affirmations. Meanwhile, affirmations and their connection to simple, everyday language influence mantras.

How Mantras Work

You already know that mantras are based on energy. However, at this point you may be wondering how exactly they work. How can reciting a word, phrase, or sound actually transform you?

It turns out that what you think has a big impact on your overall health and well-being. For example, if you think a negative thought, such as *I have no time*, your bodily systems will react. Both your nervous and respiratory systems will speed up, causing anxiety, setting your heart racing, and so on. When you repeat these kinds of thoughts out loud, you are fertilizing them with sound. This, in turn, depletes your energy levels. Once in that depleted state, the chances are you will revisit these same words, phrases, and comments later on. And around you'll go again. This cycle increases the likelihood you will develop unconscious beliefs and behaviors (thinking, wanting, trying, fixing) as an attempt to control this loss of energy. Sounds pretty exhausting, huh? Fortunately, it doesn't have to be this way.

Mantras allow you to take charge of your energy. Directing your energy to a positive, thoughtful place can help you reduce stress—and we all know the negative effects stress has on a body. In fact, the Mayo Clinic endorses positive thinking and self-talk because it may:

- Increase your life span
- Lower rates of depression
- Help you de-stress
- Give you greater resistance to the common cold
- Improve your overall psychological and physical well-being

- Reduce your risk of death from cardiovascular disease
- Give you better coping skills during life's obstacles

Mantras are a great way to engage in positive self-talk. They have an effortless way of aiding you to surrender struggle, release control, and become fully engaged in the present moment.

> "You never have to change what you
> see, only the way you see it."
>
> Thaddeus Golas, *The Lazy Man's Guide to Enlightenment*

Benefits of Mantras

When practiced regularly, mantras are like medicine for your energy. According to *Healing Mantras*, "mantras help prepare your energy centers (chakras) to receive and use large amounts of spiritual energy." Think of the energy in your body like a lightbulb. You can have a 25-, 50-, or 100-watt bulb, depending on how much energy you have. The more you utilize mantras, the more wattage (energy) your lightbulb (body) is able to hold.

Some additional benefits of reciting mantras include the following.

RELEASING SUBCONSCIOUS EMOTIONS

According to kundalini yoga as taught by Yogi Bhajan, when you tap the roof of your mouth with your tongue—as you do when chanting some of the seed sounds—you release emotions from the part of your brain called the hypothalamus. This occurs through repetitive action. As you'll learn next, traditional mantra practice often includes a minimum of 108 repetitions. Therefore, when repeating a seed sound such as RAM, you may not feel an emotional release until you have paused at the end of 30, 50, or 108 reps. You know you are releasing stress and subconscious emotions when your body takes in a fresh, deep inhale, a bodily sigh, or makes a deep, relaxing exhale.

Even an action as simple as repeating the syllable *la, la, la* touches your tongue to the roof of your mouth. Go ahead and try it right now. Perhaps this is one of the many reasons singing can lift your mood and attitude. Notice how your energy becomes light and playful.

INCREASING CALM

Breathing is such an important part of finding and maintaining a sense of calm. And mantras have a way of getting you to pay attention to your breathing. Think about it: It's impossible to inhale when you are speaking words or phrases. At the end of the phrase, especially if it was a long one, you can feel your body automatically taking an inhale.

What was previously reported as "junk" DNA is now being seen by some scientists as DNA with a higher purpose. As it turns out, you have DNA that hasn't even been activated yet. Pretty cool, huh? According to author Brendan D. Murphy, one of the ways to activate this DNA is through vowel chants, *a e i o u*. German authors Grazyna Fosar and Franz Bludorf are studying DNA activation ideas through mantras as well. These concepts are in their infancy, but offer some promising opportunities!

Mantras that get you to extend your exhale are especially great for training your body to breathe properly. You see this when you chant a sound such as *ha, ha, ha, ha, ha* continuously. As soon as you stop, your lower belly fills up with air (inhales) quite effortlessly. Whenever you are breathing from your lower abdomen (inhale inflating the belly, exhale deflating) you are stimulating the lower lobes of your lungs, which is where all the calming nerves are located.

CHANGING YOUR BRAIN FOR THE BETTER

Mantras not only stimulate the right and left sides of your brain, but repetitive usage of mantras can alter brain waves from a beta state (when you are super focused) to a more theta state (relaxed). Theta states raise your level of awareness and consciousness, providing a sense of calm and ease.

For example, the sound of *Om*, which is often recited in yoga classes, balances beta (focused), theta (relaxed), and delta (dreamlike) states, helping you to feel more calm and open. This openness is how you know you are connected to your soul. Your soul carries the memory of love. As a result, you feel supported and present.

INCREASING HEALTH, AWARENESS, AND UNIVERSAL CONNECTION

Balancing your brain waves through mantras not only makes you feel better overall but also connects you to a universal intelligence, where deep healing and transformation occur. If you are wondering what that means for you, the history of mantras (particularly the ones in Sanskrit) is noted as being a means for clearing up negative karma, which some believe may contribute to current negative emotional and physical experiences. Universal intelligence is what the book *The Secret* is based on. The idea is that you are in constant communication with the spiritual laws of the universe—one being the law of karma, which affirms "for every action there is a reaction." Mantras are a way to clear up negative actions, opening up new pathways for positive ones.

How to Use a Mantra

Although mantras are simply words or phrases to repeat, there is an art to practicing them most effectively. Here are some tips for integrating mantras into your everyday life.

CREATE A SACRED SPACE

Having a sacred space helps you commit to and develop the ritual of a mantra practice. You may select a special chair that looks out a window, or perhaps you might go somewhere outdoors where you can relax. Your sacred space doesn't have to be fancy, but it can be fun and creative. Some people like to put together a small altar (or shelf) in their home and place sacred items on it, such as spiritual statues, candles, crystals, chimes, incense, or pictures. My altar sits next to a chair in my office, and on it I have a display of crystals and special rocks I found at the beach. When it is nice outside, I often bring my mantra practice out to my back deck, where I can chant and watch the birds eat from the birdfeeder. You can also use a meditation cushion or a prayer bench, if it feels right to you.

PRONOUNCE THEM PROPERLY

Before beginning to use a mantra, it is helpful to know the difference between reciting a mantra and chanting it. Reciting means to state something out loud a few times, while chanting means to continually repeat something out loud for a long period of time, at least five minutes. Since mantras are energy focused, it is important that you take the time to learn them properly before chanting. Before you chant a mantra, recite it first so that you can be sure you are pronouncing it correctly, and so you can get comfortable with the words and sounds. Many of the Sanskrit mantras can be found on YouTube if you need help learning how to say them.

PRACTICE FREQUENCY

According to ancient tradition, the Sanskrit mantras should be chanted for a minimum of 108 times per day for forty days. For example, if you know someone who is severely ill, you might chant 108 times in the morning and 108 times in the evening.

If that amount of chanting sounds daunting, don't worry. As you will discover when you begin your practice with daily mantras using this book, you can repeat them as often as you feel comfortable. The text accompanying certain mantras will give you more guidance on this. The bottom line: It is best to repeat whatever mantra you are drawn to as many times as you want.

You may also consider using a few mantras in your daily language at your chosen frequency, and also selecting one or two Sanskrit mantras that you will commit to chanting for a minimum of forty days.

CHANT YOUR MANTRAS INTENTIONALLY

What makes a mantra effective is not so much the words themselves (although they are very powerful) but rather your relationship with the mantra itself. To develop this relationship, it is important to consider many aspects of how you engage in the mantra: your tone of voice, whether you want or need to pause, the energy you feel in your body, and how you feel about the experience. Think of it as being similar to telling a story to one of your friends. To really communicate and get your point across, you might use an inflection in your voice—you might pause, reflect, or change the volume of your voice. Also, know you are not controlling the mantra. Your breath will feel shallow because you are chanting the words on exhale. When you pause it is likely you will receive a nice inhale. Think of it like taking a sip out of a straw, allowing yourself to really get a taste.

BELIEVE IN YOUR WORDS

When I teach, I tell my students, "You cannot choose what you don't believe in." Some of you may have trouble stating these mantras at first because you feel you are not worthy of the kind of love that these mantras express. Yet, if you don't believe in love, you cannot choose it, nor can you truly choose happiness, health, and prosperity. You have to believe it to choose it and one of the ways to increase your ability to believe in yourself and your dreams is to increase the vibration of the energy within you. Mantras can do this for you.

INCORPORATE MANTRAS INTO YOUR DAILY SCHEDULE

While it's nice to have special time set aside every day to chant your mantras, this isn't always possible. Don't let a busy schedule stop you from beginning your practice. Instead, find a way to work mantras into your schedule and lifestyle. Mantra practices blend easily into other practices and routines, such as a yoga class, prayer, tai chi, walking, journaling, and gardening. If you can't work mantras into one of those types of activities, try to find mental space at an otherwise "lost" time, such as during your commute or while washing dishes. Two simple words, such as *thank you*, can be the mantra you state before meals, or it can be the mantra you use to begin your day. (As you will see, mantras are also a great way to let go at the end of a day!)

SAY THANK YOU

Conclude each mantra with "thank you." The words *thank you* help you build the relationship with the mantra. Just like you communicate with people, mantras communicate with the universe. When you say "thank you," you are letting the universe know that you have received the energy of this mantra. "Thank you" is a gesture of appreciation. In this case, you are saying "thank you" to the universe for putting this mantra into full motion (as it has already occurred). Saying "thank you" at the end of the mantra is no different than saying, *I have full faith this is in motion.*

Moving Forward in Your Practice: Mala Beads, Mudras, and Kirtan

As you become more comfortable with mantras, you might want to take your commitment to the next level. The following ideas can help you do just that.

PURCHASE MALA BEADS

Mala beads are a string of 108 beads that are used as a tool for keeping track of how many mantras you've recited. That way you don't have to count in your head while you chant. These beads allow you to fully experience the meditative qualities a mantra can bring. Mantra beads can run anywhere from $10–$80, depending on whether they are made of seeds or crystals. I prefer crystals, as they hold electromagnetic energy. Combining the energy of the crystals and the mantra can really help you raise your vibration. Crystals, like mantras, also correspond to different parts of the body and serve different purposes. For example, I have mantra beads made out of amethyst, which is connected to your brow point (third eye). When in balance, the third eye can increase mental clarity and intuition. Amethyst is known for bringing emotional stability and psychic protection and increasing intution. This makes it a great choice for managing addiction and honing spiritual development. On the outside, addiction is a condition where one is hooked on a substance or behavior. From an energetic standpoint, addiction can be energy that has overextended itself (meaning, it is too wide open) and as a result, the person may have difficulty turning away from negative influences and choices. The combination of chanting and holding amethyst can be a powerful duo for overcoming these tendencies. As always, when it comes to choosing mala beads, the rule of thumb is to pick the one you are drawn to. Trust your body.

USE A MUDRA

You may have seen pictures of people meditating with their legs crossed and their hands in a certain position. That's what doing a mudra looks like. Mudras are hand gestures often used to complement a mantra practice, and they are powerful means for connecting to a higher consciousness. One simple mudra you can try is the hand gesture that makes something similar to the "okay" sign. Take your pointer finger and press it against your thumb. This is a universal mudra that represents the universal soul connecting with the individual soul.

Finally, mantras can be chanted to live music in a group setting with a call-and-response format. This is called a Kirtan. One person leads the group, chanting the mantra, and then the group responds with the same chant. The energy in a Kirtan can be very strong, liberating, and soothing at the same time. You can find Kirtans at your local yoga studios and retreat centers.

Writing Your Own Mantras

Writing your own mantra can sound appealing, but it is trickier than you think. The key is to center yourself through breathing and connecting to the present moment before jotting down ideas. To be effective, mantras should be written as if the intended situation is already happening. For this reason, you should use present-tense language. One of the most powerful mantras you can write and state is "I am."

It is easy to get caught up in wanting your mantra to sound flowery, or in trying to make it rhyme perfectly. Avoid those temptations and instead focus on communicating with the universe as well as your subconscious mind. Focus on what you want to create, rather than on rhymes or adjectives.

Sharing Mantras with Others

When you begin to realize the power of mantras, you'll probably want to share it with friends and family. You may be tempted to give others prescriptive advice about mantras. *Just do this or say this and it will all be better!* Resist that urge and instead simply share your own experiences with a mantra. Rather than tell other people what to do, show them how mantras have affected your life. You can also share mantras through music. See the Website Resources section at the end of this book for some suggestions.

You Deserve This

Mantras lift your energy up enough so that you can pause and remember who you are. If you are surprised by this or somehow feel undeserving of such grace, I assure you that mantras are already a part of your core essence. Their energy is made up of the very same energy you're made of. Yet mantras, when used effectively, do not contain the lower-energy daily hassles, fears, and insecurities. They are pure, and because of that, reciting and receiving the energy of a mantra is no different than being blessed. Mantras honor your soul's journey by recognizing you as an endless creator and source of infinite love.

2

MANTRAS
FOR HAPPINESS

"There is no path to happiness;
happiness is the path."

Gautama Buddha

Mantras are one of the simplest ways to reach and maintain states of happiness. One of the ways they do this is by neutralizing unhappiness. To neutralize means to take the charge (reactivity) out. For example, someone may say to themselves, "I feel happy at work but unhappy in my marriage." As a result, that person may compare, judge, or complain about one versus the other. The truth of the matter is that the individual probably feels more energetically stuck in fear (charge) in the marriage than at work. People cannot make us feel certain emotions; they are revealed to us (meaning, the emotions already existed). A marriage may reveal fearful emotions that have existed for years.

Mantras can help you transform fearful states into more useful ones, like clarity. Once this energy is unleashed, it uplifts you to more productive states of mind. Someone who is unsure about her marriage will be able to see the situation more clearly, and rather than stay stuck (which could look like ranting about the situation), she will be able to move forward (e.g., get support, communicate). The wonderful part about mantra practices is they uplift all areas of your life, not just the ones you think are bad or frustrating. With consistency and dedication, don't be surprised if reciting a mantra for your marriage also improves the quality of your worklife.

The mantras in this chapter are based on the qualities scientifically proven to generate happiness, such as your ability to be present, open to joy, and compassionate to self and others. When you are in a state of happiness, you are not trying to change the moment. Instead, you find yourself actually enjoying the moment, which then allows you to interact with the world around you. For example, you may be walking down a street and decide to spontaneously stop and pet a dog. Immediately, you feel happy. Mantras can help you achieve that state of happiness.

Furthermore, according to the organization Project Happiness, a full 90 percent of our happiness is based on our "inner environment," which is made up of our genes and our intentional activities, like self-reflection, mindfulness, and gratitude. Mantras help you shape your "inner environment" and sustain your own happiness.

As I expand my awareness, energy flows freely through me.

It can be so easy to get caught up in other people's descriptions of happiness. A Facebook post, bit of celebrity news, or Snapchat photo compels you to live someone else's moment (even if it is fixed or filtered or edited), and it can give you a false impression of what true happiness is. When you overfocus on other people as a measure of your own happiness, you inevitably disconnect from your source of happiness—yourself. Happiness is an internal state of being, not an external place you have to find. Recite this mantra to redirect and expand your awareness to your internal source of happiness.

I am a part of something greater.
My breath unites me with this now.

Abraham Maslow, a famous psychologist, was one of the first to recognize the importance of developing a sense of belonging. By nature, human beings need to feel connected to others. This connection is a necessary daily supplement to fostering intellectual, physical, and emotional growth.

Naturally, there may be times when you question how and in what ways you fit in. Perhaps you are a new mom, a student, or newly retired. This uneasiness can even happen within your own family unit. Wanting, trying to "fit" in or feeling badly for being different often makes things worse. Instead, know that you are always a key part of the universe. You are wanted and needed. This mantra reminds you that you are part of something greater. It connects you to your wholeness (by saying *I am*).

I give myself permission to prioritize the things that bring me joy, creativity, and connection.

At times, you might lose your sense of direction or wonder if your life choices are off base. For example, you may crave a different lifestyle or a compatible companion. This mantra reminds you that perhaps these doubts mean that you are being connected to your divine purpose. Your creative energy can stimulate healthy change and lead to happy experiences. So allow yourself to feel these doubts, and ask yourself if they could become motivation for you to reclaim happiness. Rather than focus on what is missing from your life, this mantra encourages you to incorporate things that bring you joy (e.g., animals, nature, art, music, etc.).

I align myself with happiness.

This mantra reminds you that you get to choose what you are aligned with. You can either become aligned with love or fear. To align yourself more closely and consistently with love, call upon your imagination. According to Albert Einstein, "Imagination is more powerful than knowledge." This is because your body does not know the difference between reality and fantasy. If you imagine as if you are feeling happy and content, your body will pick up on this and create the experience for you.

Neuroscience supports this strategy, acknowledging the powerful benefits of visualization. These types of tools (visualization, breathing) allow you to tap into unexpressed energy and transform it into moments of inspiration.

I am blessed.

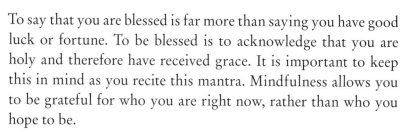

To say that you are blessed is far more than saying you have good luck or fortune. To be blessed is to acknowledge that you are holy and therefore have received grace. It is important to keep this in mind as you recite this mantra. Mindfulness allows you to be grateful for who you are right now, rather than who you hope to be.

Another version of this mantra is "We are blessed." This statement gives you the ability to see and honor the grace in others.

I receive fully the joy and nourishment nature brings.

Some of your "happy chemicals" include serotonin and dopamine. Mantras not only support the production of these chemicals; they also shift your brain waves into more calming states. A March 2014 article in the magazine *Psychology Today* noted that "nature relatedness often predicts happiness regardless of other psychological factors." This mantra is great for those times of day when you are transitioning from indoors to outdoors (e.g., checking your mail or walking to your car). It encourages you to fully soak in the ample benefits nature provides.

Appreciation and gratitude pulsate through me now.

Simple acts of kindness, such as holding the door for someone, letting someone go ahead of you in line, or paying for another person's cup of coffee are ways to spread happiness. Happiness is contagious. You can literally change the climate of a room through acts of kindness. As you recite this mantra, notice how the energy of the words rests on your heart. Breathe deeply as you send loving thoughts to yourself and the world around you.

**Energy flows where attention goes.
I choose to focus on bliss.**

Happiness and joy are experiences. Research shows that individuals who prioritize experiences over purchases tend to be happier. Before reciting this mantra, take a moment to close your eyes and soften the muscles in your face and shoulders. Ask your body what brings it joy. Pause and notice what comes up for you. Perhaps you'll imagine a place you like to visit, certain people in your life, listening to music, or spending time in nature. Visualize these things as you recite this mantra several times.

My awareness is enough.

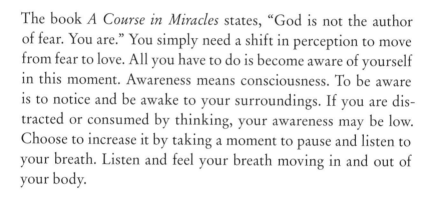

The book *A Course in Miracles* states, "God is not the author of fear. You are." You simply need a shift in perception to move from fear to love. All you have to do is become aware of yourself in this moment. Awareness means consciousness. To be aware is to notice and be awake to your surroundings. If you are distracted or consumed by thinking, your awareness may be low. Choose to increase it by taking a moment to pause and listen to your breath. Listen and feel your breath moving in and out of your body.

I believe in my abilities and strengths.

According to a March 2014 *Psychology Today* article, focusing on your strengths decreases depression and increases healthy behaviors such as an active lifestyle. In order to focus on your strengths, you must first recognize what they are. Ask yourself two questions:

1. In what areas do I feel strong?
2. In what areas am I getting stronger?

These areas can be as simple as feeling strong in a particular skill such as cooking, drawing, or reading. You may have strong interpersonal skills, or maybe you are pretty good at getting organized or using a computer. Take a moment now to acknowledge what you are good at as well as the skills you look forward to developing.

I am a contributor to my community.

Your soul wants to contribute to something greater than you. As a human being, you can have everything—all the money and fame—however, if you do not feel like you are contributing to the world in some way, you will feel unsatisfied. Taking time to contribute to your surroundings can change all of this. Whether it be taking a moment to pick up a piece of trash, donating a few items, or volunteering at a local charity, contributing to your community not only helps other people but also makes you happier. In fact, according to Sara Konrath, PhD, a faculty member of the Research Center for Group Dynamics at the University of Michigan, "volunteering is associated with lower depression, increased well-being, and a 22 percent reduction in the risk of dying." Do you need more reasons than those?

I smile big, even when no one is looking.

It takes many more muscles to make a frown than it does to make a smile. Smiling (even if you fake it) can improve your mood, which makes it a lot easier to generate happy thoughts. If you are wondering how this works, try checking yourself out while smiling in the mirror. When you smile, your eyes light up. Now notice the difference when a flat expression is on your face. Even if you don't feel much like smiling today, try getting out in the world and taking a look around. Watching children or animals or sitting in nature has a wonderful way of bringing a smile to your face. Some happy thoughts might just follow.

Things always work out for me.

There have been so many times in my life when this mantra has given me the strength to believe in something, even if there is no proof. Perhaps you are waiting to hear about a job offer, hoping to get into a particular college, or maybe you are supporting a loved one through a rough situation. Choose to believe everything will (and has always) worked out for you and everyone else. See yourself as resilient and strong. Remember, saying something as if it is true and happening is very powerful.

Happiness is a feeling; joy is an experience. I choose both.

Happiness is a feeling that makes you feel lighthearted and allows you to experience pleasure. Like other emotions, happiness can have a range. On one end, you can be elevated, perhaps giddy, while on the other end, you may feel quietly content. One is not better than the other; both are experiences of happiness. Joy tends to be less dependent on situations or circumstances. Joy is a state of being. Sure, you might have moments where you feel sad or even angry, but those emotions do not destroy your overall joy for living.

Beautiful inside and out.

Beauty is much more than skin deep. Someone may be attractive on the outside, yet be riddled with insecurity, hatred, and jealousy on the inside. This can make him or her challenging to be around, and it may be difficult to maintain a relationship with this person. True beauty happens when it is illuminated through you; when your happiness, love, and contentment shine through your speech and actions.

According to the website WebMD, being stressed all the time can actually deprive you of vital nutrients necessary for sustaining physical health. Stress can negatively affect the vitality of your skin and hair, and can even cause high blood pressure, headaches, and stomachaches. Incorporating mantras into your life is one way to de-stress and ensure beauty, inside and out.

I am a happy soul.

So many people try to be a happy human. Fair enough. But I say, focus on being a happy *soul*. Happy souls have no problem asking for guidance and support. Unhappy souls feel alone, unsupported, and disconnected. The next time you feel unsure about what to do, rather than ask your brain, ask your soul. "Soul, what would you have me do?" Your soul speaks to you through a hunch or a feeling, sometimes even visually or auditorily. Embrace each as a message guiding you toward a happy life.

I have something good to say and I choose to say it!

Have you ever had a positive or kind thought and held yourself back from sharing it? Perhaps you loved a yoga class but never took the time to express it to the teacher, or you were touched by the kind gesture of another but felt awkward letting her know.

Giving other people compliments or thanking them for their time and attention brings happiness to both parties. Let's face it, even the most confident people could use a pat on the back now and then. Make a point to let others know they are doing a good job and watch how *your* happiness increases too!

Shine on!

Happy people tend to *shine on* rather than *move on*. To *move on* means to push your feelings down or hold them back, and then go about your way. To *shine on* means to pause and allow yourself to fully experience what is coming up without judging it. You might feel a twisted feeling in your stomach, tightness in your chest, or clenching of your teeth. Shining on means to trust the inner guidance of your body. Digest your emotions and you will grow (shine) from the experience. Ignore or guard yourself from your emotions and you may find yourself recycling (stuck in) the same emotions and experiences.

3

MANTRAS TO OVERCOME FEAR AND ANXIETY

"Love is what we are born
with. Fear is what we learn."

Marianne Williamson

Fear and anxiety sap your energy and happiness. Think of it like when your computer is running sluggishly—it still works, but the programs take forever to load. Fear in the body works the same way. You have energy, but it is heavy and congested. All your body's energy vibrates, but fearful energy vibrates at a low level because it's not circulating properly. Your body may be hanging on to unconscious memories, beliefs, and feelings that are fearful in nature. When left unresolved, over time these fears can manifest into physical and emotional conditions, such as chronic worry, nervousness, tension, headaches, back pain, and more.

Mantras can change the story from fearful to fearless. They do this by digging deep into the root system of fearful stories, beliefs, and thoughts. As the energy of these mantras begins to enter your body, don't be put off if you feel some discomfort.

Discomfort is a sign of growth and is an indication that old energy is transforming into something new. (Yes, contrary to what you might believe, you don't get rid of anxiety; you transform it!) You have the power to do that—and mantras are a tremendous resource.

In this chapter, you will find a variety of mantras. Some clear away what no longer serves you, while others activate dormant energy. Dormant energy is energy that has been suppressed over time, even generations. Be patient. Select two or three mantras that resonate with you and practice them daily.

Fear is an illusion. Love is the only thing that is real.

Here is the thing: Fear is not real. Yup, you heard me, fear is not real. When you are experiencing symptoms of fear it sure feels real, though, doesn't it? The way you see the world is affected when you are in fear and your energy is not circulating properly. Rather than seeing choices, you see limitations; rather than seeing love, you see hurt and resentment.

Take a few moments now to connect with your breath. On inhale, inflate your lower abdomen and take in one slow, rhythmic breath. Allow the energy of fear to transform into courage, strength, and (with practice) love. State this mantra three to five times and then take one full complete breath (inhale to the count of three and exhale to the count of three). Imagine these words as energy moving freely through your body.

I am receiving energy now.

Breathing effectively is one of the easiest ways to uplift your energy. If taking a deep breath is difficult for you, consider softening your body. You can do this in a number of places. First, relax the muscles in your face, the corners of your mouth, your shoulders, and your upper back. Now sit up tall and relax your shoulder blades. Notice if you pull down the tops of your shoulders to do this. If you did, try another method of relaxing them instead. Imagine that your shoulder blades rest on your back like wings. You can activate your wings by squeezing them toward one another (around the back of your heart). Squeeze them together and release a few times. Notice how this gently encourages your shoulders to relax while it simultaneously loosens your jaw. Movements such as this will help you get out of your head and into your body.

Remember to focus on your breathing. If focusing on your abdomen while you breathe is discouraging, try shifting your awareness to the sides of your waist or even your lower back and breathe deeply into those areas. Release the need to do things perfectly or right.

Feel everything; attach to nothing.

You might be attached to a number of beliefs or thoughts on a daily basis—these are called attachments. One of my spiritual teachers, Dr. Zoe Marae, first introduced me to this mantra. She taught me to recognize attachment as a state of nonfeeling (thinking). To feel means you are experiencing sensations in your body. Anxiety is a state of nonfeeling. Sure, you may have anxious thoughts and think about worried feelings; however, fear blocks you from actually experiencing your feelings.

After reciting this mantra, pull your navel in and squeeze out and exhale. Notice how your inhale grows stronger. Do this a few times and you will soon experience your sensations (feelings) without attachment to outcome.

Being firmly grounded into my body offers me peace.

Grounding yourself into the present moment is an essential part of transforming anxiety. Picture in your mind a large, old tree. See its strong root system and flexible branches. Picture the peacefulness of the tree and the nourishment it brings to its environment. You are no different than this tree. You also have a strong root system, capable of providing security and peace.

Very often, when you are experiencing fear, energy becomes congested in the heart area and the solar plexus (navel area). When using this mantra, soften your solar plexus (navel area) and on exhale, imagine directing your energy out through your legs into the ground. See it travel through Mother Earth, deep into the core of the planet. Allow this mantra to support your energy by grounding it into the earth through this tree visualization.

The universe generously supports me.

If you rarely ask for help and tend to take the world on your shoulders, you might want to consider getting to know this mantra. Taking on the worries and concerns without regard for yourself makes life seem heavy and challenging, rather than light and interesting. If you believe you are unsupported, the universe will reflect that back to you. Instead, recognize that your support goes far beyond the things and people around you. You also have universal support—in many ways a spiritual team—that you can access through mantras.

Now that I have released all excess stress, I am calm and peaceful.

Panic can feel like the rug is being pulled out from underneath your feet. Not all stress is bad, but sometimes you might carry a bit too much of it. If you feel panic, bring your awareness to your larger muscle groups (thighs and buttocks) and relax them. Begin to recite this mantra while placing your feet flat on the floor. You may even want to rub the tops of your thighs with the palms of your hands, kind of like a massage, while reciting it. The combination of the mantra and connecting to your large muscles will help calm you down.

I feel the flow of light now.

Worrying about the future is an energy drainer. It is a counter-productive means for attempting to control outcome. The more you attempt to control, the more stuck, emotionally fragile, and overwhelmed you may feel. Treat your body as an ally. What is it trying to tell you? Deferring to your body as a channel of light and love brings you to the present moment, where fear and worry do not exist. If you tend to focus on what you have to do or what is left undone, consider reciting this mantra at the beginning and end of each day.

It's got to be better than I think.

This mantra takes you beyond your thoughts. It reminds you that your thoughts could never capture the possibilities and magnificence that are available to you when you allow yourself to move through your feelings and detach from thinking.

This mantra was passed on to me by Zoe Marae, PhD. She described it as a way to complete what she referred to as "repeaters." Repeaters are what you can attract into your life based on old patterns. Reciting this mantra opens the doorway to new ways of being, and as this occurs new perceptions will surface. As Candace Pert, author of *Molecules of Emotion*, shares, sensations create perceptions. Utilizing this mantra gives you a much more open feeling, providing an inevitable shift in the way you see your world.

I am learning to communicate in peaceful and empowering ways.

A big part of living a fearless and happy life is learning how to communicate effectively. Mantras teach you how to become more energy-focused in your communication, rather than word-focused. Sure, words have energy, but just because you hear words that have low vibrations (e.g., "This sucks!") doesn't mean you have to react to them. Notice the energy without judgment. Rather than focusing on the meaning of the word, observe the energy. For example, if someone says "This sucks," observing the energy gives you information (guidance) that this person may feel overwhelmed or stuck in a situation. Then you can respond with, "Sounds like you feel stuck." This response is a much more effective way to free them than if you attempt to fix their issue or take on their frustration yourself.

Setting clear, healthy limits comes easily and naturally for me now.

Setting clear limits is like receiving a ticket to freedom. Limits are a way to respect the needs of yourself and others. Without boundaries, you are likely to send the universe mixed messages. Part of you may say yes, while another part of you says no.

In the beginning, this mantra might feel a little foreign or uncomfortable when you recite it. Don't let this discourage you. If you feel uncomfortable, this means you could really benefit from this one. Recite this mantra several times daily. Observe your body and breathe for a minute or two when done.

Now that courage, strength, and love are in motion, all shadows of doubt are erased.

Think of doubt as streaks on a window. They can create an unpleasant distraction from what you're trying to see outside. Doubts have the same effect on your energy—they distract it and make it congested. Use this mantra to alter the energy of doubt into courage. Similar to wiping a window clean, use this mantra to transform doubt into courage. I would suggest you sit or stand up tall when you are reciting it. Allow yourself to really feel it in your body.

Beloved body, you are safe and free.

If you tend to turn to food for comfort and relief, you may have trained your body to process your feelings through food. Food is not intended as a means to process your feelings, yet your body can start to store unresolved pain in this way. This pain eventually becomes a trigger for unworthiness, and people who store pain survive in a state of unconscious self-punishment or self-sabotage. This can be evidenced through impulsive, quick, mindless eating. If you find yourself wanting food when your body isn't hungry, take pause, state this mantra, and breathe. Recite this mantra daily as needed, particularly before and after snacks and meals.

I proclaim freedom from shock now.

Shock gives your body the ability to move through sudden disturbances, such as a death or an accident. It is your body's way of protecting you from extreme stress and anxiety. However, once the event has passed, shock can make you feel numb and stuck, making it challenging for you to be affectionate toward others.

Think of shock like a brick wall holding fear and anxiety in place. If you suspect shock may be unresolved in your body, recite this mantra, then breathe and visualize a wall slowly being dismantled.

I am protected by the golden light that surrounds me now.

Fear of flying or nervousness about travel in general can inhibit you from visiting family or exploring new places. Let this mantra ease your nerves while strengthening your energy. Consider reciting this mantra a minimum of twenty times per day several days before your flight. Close your eyes and visualize the protective light around you. The more familiar you become with this mantra ahead of time, the more powerful it becomes. Then when you use it during flight, it is more likely to bring you comfort.

I am (inhale, exhale) calm.
I can do this.

If you are nervous about speaking in front of a group of people, this mantra is for you. The words "I am" are some of the most powerful words you can use. Think of these words as putting into motion what it is you choose to create. In this case, you are activating calm by embracing nervousness. See yourself as improving and know, with practice, this fear can and will dissipate. Practice this mantra in front of a mirror and see how this strengthens you.

I am receiving strength through vulnerability.

Social anxiety is often due to a fear of being judged as well as the belief that you cannot cope with certain situations. This nervousness and worry, when left unattended, can develop into symptoms of anxiety. This mantra reminds you that the very thing you are afraid of (vulnerability) can offer you power. The act of acknowledging your vulnerability actually gives you power. When reciting this mantra, see yourself as moving from helpless to courageous.

4

MANTRAS FOR LOVE

"The love that you withhold
is the pain that you carry."

Ralph Waldo Emerson

What do mantras have to do with love? Everything! When you recite mantras, you are choosing to welcome love into your life. They don't get you to love or make some fairytale relationship happen. Mantras work through what love is: energy, vibration, and light. Since you are made of all of this as well, you are love. Mantras clear away whatever is getting in the way of you remembering this. They effortlessly pour love and light upon you, and as this occurs you get to begin the process of creating something new.

There is more love in the universe than the human mind could ever grasp. Strategies for finding love, such as wanting, trying, begging, hoping, pleading, and sometimes even dreaming, don't always pan out. If anything, they make love seem like an object, something you have or needs fixing or has just plain disappeared. Mantras gracefully steer you away from all that boloney. Think of love mantras like drinking water. Give yourself at least a minimum of eight repetitions a day. Pick one and say it eight times or choose a variety; it doesn't matter, just allow yourself to be hydrated with love.

This chapter provides you a blend of mantras, some which give you the means to love yourself more fully while others stimulate relationships and loved-based situations.

I love being me.

Being you means you are able to allow your own thoughts, feelings, and beliefs to emerge with honor and respect. This does not mean you have to act on every little thing. Notice if you start to compare yourself to others or question your abilities and strengths. Take these doubts as sign that you may be veering from your sense of being. Your path is always being shaped by the way you respond to what is happening inside of you. To get back on your course, put your attention on the now and recite this mantra.

I live and breathe in the heart of God (and/or universe).

Divine love happens when human love (your ability to sense and connect to the energy within you) and universal energy unite. Divine love is your oneness with creation. Some may call it God, while others may refer to it as the universe. How you see it is your personal choice. As long as your words come from a loving space, feel free to use whatever phrase feels most comfortable and expansive.

Believing is receiving.
I believe in love.

The more you believe in love, the more you will receive it. You cannot receive what you don't fully believe in. It is kind of like listening to a sales pitch and being on the fence as to whether you really are buying into what someone says about the product. When you don't quite buy into something completely, you might act a little guarded. So I ask you, do you believe in love? Let me tell you, the answer does not come from your head; it comes from your body (heart). Your body is a truth teller—your head, on the other hand, likes to make stuff up.

Let love grow.

It would be nice if love just grew by itself, but that is not always the case. Love doesn't automatically grow just because you have a big, fancy wedding. Love grows with awareness, insight, creativity, and a willingness to integrate practices like mantras into your daily life. The good news is that the seeds of love never die. Think of this mantra like putting a plant in the sun and watering it. This choice and commitment is your way of allowing and encouraging love to grow.

Now that I trust my energy fully and completely, love flows freely to me.

You can either dedicate your energy to love or fear. Everything that is in front of you is also inside of you. Choose to trust what your energy tells you without judgment. If you feel fear, acknowledge it but don't dwell in it. Breathe through the fear and welcome love instead. When you trust your energy, you develop a keen sense of awareness—a way to follow your heart and do what feels right.

My body is a temple rich with love and light.

As mantras permeate your energy, your light (energy) grows stronger. As this occurs, you are less likely to take things personally. This is one of the many ways you know you have begun to embody love. This is not to say you won't have reflections of insecurity or even pain; however, you are less likely to follow (think about) them. They become a momentary experience rather than a story you attach to. See your body as a temple—the holder of the love flame—as you recite this mantra.

I allow my cells to vibrate to love now.

Your cells are made of molecules and atoms in motion. Cells play a large role in your physical communication system. They are the foundation of your bodily components (e.g., muscles, glands, organs), but they also send out and receive signals from the universe. Mantras communicate with your cells through sound and vibration. Reciting this mantra communicates with the inner workings of your thoughts and feelings. Fill your cells with light and their powers of communication will grow stronger, making you happier and healthier.

I have released all negative patterns, conditions, and restrictions on love, so all pathways are now open.

"Love blocks" are conditions and counterproductive beliefs around love. Some common love blocks are beliefs that love is something you have to earn, prove, or hold on to tightly. Love can also be something that you believe you must hand over or give to others, leaving very little for yourself. These are all untruths that can block your ability to give, receive, and benefit from love. As you chant this mantra, some of these blocks are likely to surface. Let them. Breathe, stick with the chant, and allow them to leave your body. Recite as many times as you like.

Choosing to love myself comes more easily now. I am learning to listen to the needs of my body and spirit.

Overfocusing on your problems or worrying about the future disables your ability to tune in to love. If you question your relationships or expect that certain things in your life are unlikely to work out, then you will strip away at the love inside of you. Rather than continue these patterns, choose to focus on self-love. Self-love is not as complicated or overwhelming as you might think. The act of pausing and taking a drink of water is a demonstration of love. Noticing the temperature of the water as it runs over your hands while washing dishes is a way to connect to love. Love is in the moment; it is right now, as you are reading this. Pay attention to how your body responds to the experiences and interactions of your day without judgment. Soak up moments that offer you connections to the moment. These are all part of love.

Passion, I am that!

Passion gives you the ability to see the world in color. When you are focused on comparing and contrasting, you are in black-or-white (all-or-none) thinking. Black-and-white thinking narrows your focus. As this occurs, you may become tied to time and responsibilities. When you view things from passion (color) you are living in the flow (timelessness). Sure, you still get things done, but your life is fueled by your passion rather than your attachment to controlling the course of your day.

Loving myself now strengthens my ability to be a reflection of the love and strength inside others.

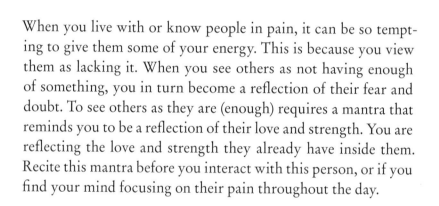

When you live with or know people in pain, it can be so tempting to give them some of your energy. This is because you view them as lacking it. When you see others as not having enough of something, you in turn become a reflection of their fear and doubt. To see others as they are (enough) requires a mantra that reminds you to be a reflection of their love and strength. You are reflecting the love and strength they already have inside them. Recite this mantra before you interact with this person, or if you find your mind focusing on their pain throughout the day.

I call upon my higher self and imagine loving you now despite our differences.

Unconditional love is being able to love yourself and others without limits or conditions. Let's face it, sometimes other people drive you crazy. You might think if they would just stop this or change that, then things would be better. When you find yourself focusing on faults more than strengths, recite this mantra. As you call on your higher self, see yourself accepting a situation you never thought you would be able to accept.

I am bursting with vitality and youth.

Love literally turns the clock back on aging. It does this by raising your endorphin levels while decreasing the production of stress hormones such as cortisol. Love is one of your highest vibrational emotions. The movement of your energy cleanses and nourishes your body, skin, mind, and internal organs. Focus on love daily, and you will activate the genes responsible for supporting your life with grace and ease.

I am mindful of my tone, speech, and actions as I choose to discipline from love and respect.

Children learn more from what we model than what we say. One of the things they learn is what you believe about love. If your tone is harsh or demeaning, kids learn to fear making mistakes. When we discipline in firm, calm, respectful tones children learn things don't have to get worse before they get better. In order to do this, it is important that you take care of yourself. This too requires discipline. Making time for yourself daily keeps your parenting skills strong and effective.

My heart leads me now;
I listen to what feels right.

Many people have been told to do one thing, but their heart steered them to another. If something feels right in your heart, it probably is right for you. In your mind, you may doubt your choices or abilities, but your heart usually gently tugs you back to what feels right. Go with this. Listen. Trust that your heart knows the way to consciousness. Your heart is highly intelligent. The more you listen, the stronger your ability to do what feels right will come through.

Love is mighty and generous.

Generosity does not come easy to everyone. If you have a hard time sharing your resources, then this may be a mantra for you to work with. Recite it daily and look for small, simple ways you can begin to share your time, energy, and resources. It can be as simple as sharing a meal. Notice what it feels like to you to be generous. Did any fears or anxieties surface? Perhaps you have a fear that there is not enough, or that somehow money and resources are limited. These fears will only force you to hold on tighter, making you feel fearful or guilty. Find an area where you can be generous, and practice it regularly along with this mantra.

The light in me sees the light in you.

This mantra is the interpretation for the word *namaste*, which is frequently stated after a meditation or yoga class. *The light in me sees the light in you* is similar to saying *the good in me sees the honorable and good in you*. When you recite this mantra, know that it does not apply exclusively to people. You can state it to a tree, animal, or even an idea. It is a gentle way to bless the world and its reflections (energetic vibrations) around you.

Love heals the source of these symptoms I am experiencing now.

Love is known for its healing qualities. Think of how healing animals and pets are—they are often brought to hospitals for patient visits. Why? Because they exude unconditional love. With this mantra, feel free to substitute "these symptoms" with the actual symptoms you are experiencing. For example, *Love heals the source of worry now* or *love heals the source for the tension in my neck and jaw now.* You can also substitute symptoms for dynamics. For example, *love heals the dynamics between my sister and me now.*

5

MANTRAS FOR FORGIVENESS AND ACCEPTANCE

"Recite mantras to cleanse the Soul.
Meditations to cleanse the Mind.
Baths to cleanse the Body."

Yogi Bhajan

Forgiveness is not an occasional act, but rather a daily practice. Forgiveness is not just the practice of forgiving but is also the practice of knowing when your body is requesting forgiveness. Just like your body sends you signals when you are hungry or tired, you also receive signals for releasing anger, resentment, and even hatred. Some of these signals may include feeling sick, unhappy, drained, and bitter. These are states of nonforgiveness. The energy of these states lacks movement, which allows them to get pent up and congested in the body. Over time, this energy congestion can lead to anxiety, depression, and illness.

Guilt and shame are also known to support nonforgiveness. You may feel guilty about a situation and unconsciously punish yourself by depriving yourself of forgiveness. Many people are uncomfortable feeling their emotions. Perhaps they witnessed unhealthy expressions of emotions in their childhood and made a silent vow that they would never allow themselves to behave in the same way. As you might have guessed, this tactic rarely works in the long haul. Eventually you will have to find ways to experience your emotions in heathy ways. Otherwise, you risk the consequence of suppressing the energy of physical and emotional pain.

Mahatma Gandhi said, "The weak can never forgive. Forgiveness is the attribute of the strong." Mantras are a comforting, harmless way to move old, congested energy so you can feel strong enough to forgive yourself or others. As this occurs, the memories that hold tight to histories of resentments and hurt begin to diminish. These memories are stored both consciously and subconsciously. Just because you are not thinking about the past doesn't mean your body isn't responding to it. Mantras are a wonderful way to release, forgive, and receive the energy that is available to you.

I accept all that is and resist nothing, as I am the energy of God.

Acceptance is so much more than letting someone into a group or tolerating differences. Acceptance is having the strength to take full responsibility for all the experiences in your life. Forgiveness and acceptance are really about taking full ownership of what you know, as well as what you might not be fully aware of. For example, someone may tell you that you hurt them deeply. You may not fully agree or be able see how you caused them harm. True acceptance means taking responsibility for the experience right in front of you despite what the evidence might look like. You may never get the physical and concrete evidence your mind is looking for, so you are better off listening to your heart (body), as it will lead you to the path of forgiveness.

I am willing and ready to take full responsibility for my actions.

As you recite this mantra, keep in mind your intention is not to admit fault but rather to restore trust and respect with another or yourself. Offering an apology is so much more than simply admitting your mistakes. A true apology gives you a way to free yourself from carrying the burden of guilt and disappointment. Sincere apologies have no alternative agenda, and are incredibly powerful energy tools for rebuilding trust and harmony.

I love you, I am sorry, please forgive me, thank you.

This Hawaiian chant (a ho'oponopono prayer chant) is an especially powerful one. When reciting this chant, you are taking full responsibility for everything that comes your way. This chant speaks to karma and how things in this life may show up due to karma in a former life. Do your best to follow the traditional mantra frequency recommendation with this one: That is, try to repeat it 108 times daily for forty days. You will benefit if you do it less, but if you are experiencing difficult circumstances or have people in your life with a lot of problems, you may want to do the full 108 times.

I choose to convert all shame to the highest vibrational light now.

Shame is one of the lowest vibrational energies in the body. It sits heavily in the body, fertilizing unworthiness and guilt. When left unattended, shame can make you feel helpless, unattractive, jealous, and insecure. Loosen the grips of shame by converting it to the lightness of high-vibrational energy. Nothing fearful can remain in this light. Allow this mantra to give you a voice for reclaiming your power. Do not let your history define you. Stating this mantra out loud to yourself will assist in releasing this emotion and all that it is attached to.

I take full responsibility for my thoughts, beliefs, feelings, and actions now.

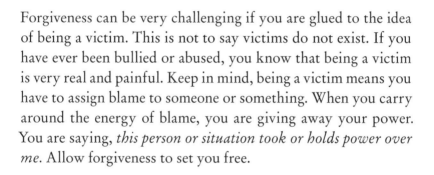

Forgiveness can be very challenging if you are glued to the idea of being a victim. This is not to say victims do not exist. If you have ever been bullied or abused, you know that being a victim is very real and painful. Keep in mind, being a victim means you have to assign blame to someone or something. When you carry around the energy of blame, you are giving away your power. You are saying, *this person or situation took or holds power over me.* Allow forgiveness to set you free.

I release through my heart center all that holds me back from truly loving and knowing my creator.

Holding on to past resentments and wounds hurts the relationship between you and your creator. As you strive to move past those resentments and strengthen that connection, don't be surprised if some of your past wounds not only dissipate but also transform into higher vibrations of love. Faith is the ultimate way to generate forgiveness. Repeat this mantra when you find yourself revisiting old stories of hurt, shame, and avoidance. After a few rounds, be sure to give your body a moment to fully exhale.

I set free the energy that tangles you with me.

We don't really let go of people; we let go of energy. Sure, your "story" with this person is the glue that ties you together. But it is the energy behind the story that keeps the dynamics in place. Think of these dynamics as strings of energy. By disentangling yourself from the story, you are setting the individuals affected (as well as yourself) free. When reciting this mantra, visualize imaginary ties kind of like knotted fishing lines slowly releasing from your heart.

I call on the blessing of divine grace for forgiveness now.

Grace works off divine mercy and, when combined with our free will, has the power to free us from burdens. Forgiveness is a privilege. It releases you from negative karma while opening your heart to receiving love. By calling on grace, you are asking for your creator to lift you from the heaviness of carrying a burden. Be sure to breathe while stating this mantra. After your exhale, pause and sit quietly.

I choose to let go by moving in rather than moving on.

When it comes to forgiveness, there is no moving on; there is only moving in. Your attitude and life experiences may change, but it is only when you move deeper into yourself that you will truly be liberated. The next time you hear yourself saying *I need to move on* or *if only I could just stop thinking about this person or situation*, consider reciting this mantra. Allow it to draw your awareness inward. As you move inward, your perception will shift and you may realize that there was never anything to let go of in the first place. The thing you thought you needed to let go of turns into something you have learned to appreciate and respect.

I align myself with this choice now.

If you are holding on to perceived faults and mistakes, somehow you may have turned yourself into the mistake. This can be a learned behavior from childhood. Somewhere along the line (perhaps school), you might have learned that mistakes are a sign of weakness or being bad. To grow and learn from your past experiences, replace the word *mistakes* with *choices*. Rather than see a situation as a mistake, instead choose to align yourself with the new choice. For example, see yourself as growing, capable, and happy and then state, *I align myself with this choice now.*

I bow to the wisdom
that reveals itself now.

Saying sorry to yourself may seem like a good thing to do, particularly if you have been a bit hard on yourself lately. Self-criticism can be very cutting to the human spirit. Getting stuck feeling sorry for what you have done to yourself or others can evoke feelings of distress and sorrow. In the long run, this may never serve you as well as you think it will. Rather than say sorry to yourself, bow to the wisdom that reveals itself through you now. Your body already knows the truth; it doesn't need you to emotionally beat yourself up about it. This mantra invites you to be grateful that you have the awareness to know your truths.

I am forgiveness in action.

A part of forgiveness rarely recognized or discussed is giving yourself permission to return to living in the present moment instead of dwelling on the past choice. Letting yourself return to the present moment is what forgiveness looks like in action. If you are caught up in the past, or nervous about the future, your energy will reflect that. The more present you are, the more energetic movement you have. This movement of your inner energy releases the confinements of past experiences.

I am that.

Moving through old wounds, habits, and negative situations can be draining. This mantra calls on your higher energy to uplift and restore you. You are an energetic being and this mantra reminds you of that. Breathe deeply before and after you recite this mantra. Do this five or six times in a row, closing your eyes and breathing deep into your core (lower abdomen area), inflating your abdomen on inhale and deflating on exhale. You really are that!

I now have the energy and strength to create new thoughts and beliefs.

Forgiveness is one of the most powerful ways to gain energy. Think of it as putting on an oxygen mask in a depressurized environment. At first it might feel awkward or even nerve-racking, but once the oxygen starts flowing, you feel alert, replenished, and free. See this mantra as a way to lift your energy either before or after you practice forgiveness. Without it, you may find yourself falling back into your old ways of seeing things.

Celebrating me today!

There are many things we celebrate in life. Babies, milestones, birthdays, etc. This mantra reminds you to take time to acknowledge your growth, even if it was small in your eyes. Something as simple as choosing to shut off your phone to receive some privacy may be a huge step. Today, celebrate your strength and willingness to forgive yourself and others. See the honor and courage required in these actions.

I release all unforgiving thoughts supported by the collective consciousness.

This mantra speaks to what divides us from oneness: religion, politics, and cultural viewpoints. Having the freedom to choose your religion and vote for whom you believe would best serve your country is a privilege. However, if you find yourself getting caught up in collective belief systems that foster negativity, anger, and even hate, you may begin to feel the negative impact of this collective consciousness. This is not to say unity isn't important, but respecting differences is critical to our evolution. This mantra will help you release that negativity.

6
MANTRAS FOR HEALING

"Therefore I tell you, whatever
you ask for in prayer, believe
that you have received
it, and it will be yours."

Mark 11:24

Healing is defined as making oneself whole again. Helping yourself heal might be as much a mental process as a physical one. Mind-body science has confirmed that if you focus on being broken, weak, or damaged, you can negatively influence your beliefs about healing. In turn, such negative influences have been proven to slow down or in some cases alter the course of healing treatments. On the other hand, research of the placebo effect shows the power of the mind to heal. Author Lissa Rankin, in *Mind Over Medicine*, states: "Nearly half of asthma patients get symptom relief from a fake inhaler or sham acupuncture. Approximately 40 percent of people with headaches get relief when given a placebo." Research cited in a November 2013 edition of the journal *Nature* discusses whether happiness can boost your immune system and make you healthier.

Think of your body like a sponge, absorbing the terms and mindsets you are exposed to. We're all familiar with some of the terms used often in the healthcare industry: pain management, illness, chronic, debilitating, precaution, and preventive measure. These terms may be helpful in gathering information for an initial diagnosis, but when they spill over into treatment they can actually interfere with your body's natural healing abilities.

The mantras in this section are specifically designed to support you in your healing journey. They are based on the science of mind-body healing and can be applied to a variety of situations. As always, do what feels right for you. Remember, mantra practices are powerful. Just because you may not see the results immediately doesn't mean your practice is not working. Stay committed and listen to your body.

Ahhhhh, (inhale, exhale)
Ahhhhhhh, (inhale, exhale)
Ahhhhhhh.

This simple sound is far more powerful than you may think. You're giving yourself permission to release that pain in your neck (or anywhere else!). Muscle tension is often a reflection of energy that is being held hostage in the body. As a result, the body becomes depleted of oxygen. Circulating fresh oxygen deep into your body helps you release this pent-up energy. Go ahead, fill your belly up with breath. Inflate it now, fully (like a balloon). Allow your mouth to open slightly and release a nice *Ahhhhh* sound.

Now that my love circuits are turned on fully, healing happens automatically for me.

Love doesn't happen *to* you; it happens *through* you. Love is a perpetual motion. Even when you can't feel love, it is still there. All you have to do is put your awareness and attention into the present moment and your love circuits become electrified. Healing is a byproduct of love. Choosing to focus on love is not different than choosing to focus on healing. When you are in the space of love, you are also experiencing healing.

Raising my awareness transcends these sensations now.

Living in pain, whether it is emotional or physical, can lead to random and sometimes impulsive thinking. Thoughts such as *I am in so much pain, my head is killing me, I feel exhausted, I need aspirin,* and *I feel like crap* can really weaken your overall well-being. The following passage is a good reminder of just how powerful our words are: "The words of the reckless pierce like a sword, but the tongue of the wise brings healing" (Proverbs 12:18). Rather than focus on the pain, instead put your attention on transcending your thoughts and words.

I am making movement count.

Sometimes you can heal minor discomforts through exercise. The American Heart Association says we should get at least 150 minutes per week of moderate exercise or 75 minutes per week of vigorous exercise (or a combination of moderate and vigorous activity). Thirty minutes a day, five times a week is an easy goal to remember. This cardio can be done in a variety of ways, such as walking, taking an exercise class, or riding a stationary bike. Simple changes such as parking your car farther away from the store or taking the stairs instead of the elevator can also boost your heart rate. If you need support for getting motivated, you might consider joining a walking group or hiring a personal trainer. Be sure to incorporate some stretching and strength training into your routine. Do what it takes to make movement count today.

Breathing in and breathing out.

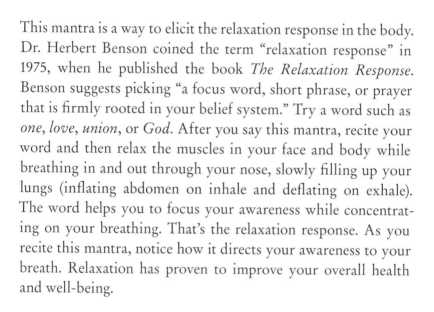

This mantra is a way to elicit the relaxation response in the body. Dr. Herbert Benson coined the term "relaxation response" in 1975, when he published the book *The Relaxation Response.* Benson suggests picking "a focus word, short phrase, or prayer that is firmly rooted in your belief system." Try a word such as *one, love, union,* or *God.* After you say this mantra, recite your word and then relax the muscles in your face and body while breathing in and out through your nose, slowly filling up your lungs (inflating abdomen on inhale and deflating on exhale). The word helps you to focus your awareness while concentrating on your breathing. That's the relaxation response. As you recite this mantra, notice how it directs your awareness to your breath. Relaxation has proven to improve your overall health and well-being.

Now that my white blood cells and spleen are thriving, I am healthy, strong, and at peace.

If you or someone you know has an autoimmune disease, such as diabetes or Lyme disease, then you've seen the challenges it can bring. Moving through such health challenges can seem like a nonstop fight. It is not uncommon to hear someone say they are "beating" or "fighting" cancer. Rather than fight with your body, this mantra invites you to make peace with it. This does not, however, imply you have to settle with your current circumstances. Making peace simply means to give up the fighting, while breathing and allowing your body to heal.

**My body is heavy, my breath is soft,
and I release myself into the arms
of God and the archangels, now.**

Being sick, hurt, or unhealthy—whether mentally or physically—can be very stressful. Sometimes it is harder to watch someone you love go through the hardship that health challenges bring. Sleep is essential to the recovery process. It gives your body the necessary downtime so that you can recover. Recite this mantra before you go to sleep. Allow it to give you the courage and strength to hand yourself over to something greater. Feel free to replace the words "God and the archangels" with another source of your choosing.

I breathe in peace,
I breathe out excess stress.

Let's get this straight: Not all stress is bad. In fact, stress is a normal, natural, and necessary part of life. But if your thoughts are predominately stressful in nature, or you find you are no longer enjoying life due to excessive thinking and pressure, then consider reciting this mantra. Allow it to shift you gently back to your most natural state of balance and ease. Be sure to breathe as you state this mantra to yourself out loud. See your breath as beautiful colors (yellows, blues, and greens) gently moving in and out of your body.

I live in harmony with the universe.

To live with disease or affliction means to live in disharmony. The spiritual law of harmony explains how the universe naturally wants to balance itself out. Since you are made of energy, and you are part of this amazing universe, you (and your body) work the same way. When you are sick, you are living in a state of imbalance. Your body craves balance and wants to return to harmony, in accordance with this law. Help it restore balance with this mantra. Keep in mind, balance looks different to all human beings. Since we all come from different backgrounds and histories, it is best not to judge how "balance" is expressed by you as compared to anyone else.

I allow the trillions of cells within me to vibrate at the highest, healthiest level possible, and so it is.

Notice how the purpose of this mantra is to repair, yet the words imply that the healing is already happening. As you recite this mantra, imagine it is happening exactly in that moment. You are transforming your cells, and by doing so you are encouraging your energy to vibrate faster. Recite this mantra if you are experiencing inflammation (e.g., back pain and/or arthritis pain). You can also recite it if you are feeling high levels of stress, which can cause inflammation in the body.

Having my tissues, glands, organs, cells, and skin rinsed of all impurities replenishes me now.

Toxins are chemicals in the environment that can compromise your immune system. Toxins can be found in food, water, and air. Pesticides, pollution, and chemicals are some of the most common toxins people encounter in their daily lives. Your body has likely adjusted to the majority of them. However, if you feel sensitive to chemicals, this mantra may be for you. State it when you are in the bathtub or shower or before you drink a nice glass of water. Allow the mantra to penetrate the water as it cleanses, relaxes, and hydrates your body.

I live well.

To be well, you have to live well. Rather than focusing on what you can't do, or your limitations, this mantra reminds you that you are both the author and the illustrator of your life. Before repeating it, ask yourself what does living well look like for me? How does it feel? What would I imagine myself doing if I were living well? Repeat this mantra several times and allow yourself to visualize what this would look, feel, and sound like.

I am a healer.

Everyone is a healer. You may not choose to be a healer for a living, but you still have the ability to heal yourself and others. Healers use energy, insight, and higher consciousness—the very same things you are made of—to facilitate wellness. Your hands are like magnets that can (with knowledge and practice) move energy. Small gestures, such as placing your hand on your heart or your forehead, are innate healing behaviors.

You have to feel it to heal it.

Anxiety and depression can hurt. Not only do they give you emotional symptoms such as nervousness and sadness, they also show up as physical symptoms such as neck pain, fatigue, and backache. Thinking or hiding these feelings may hinder your healing potential. To feel means to give yourself permission to experience an emotion (e.g., worry) from beginning, middle, to end. The best way to do this is through mindful breathing. One simple tip is to actually count as you breathe (as you inhale and exhale). To do that, inflate your belly to the count of three, and on exhale deflate your lower abdomen to the count of three. Initially, it may seem awkward, but with practice you will begin to experience the power of mind-body healing.

I can always count on my instincts and intuition.

If you find yourself trying to make yourself go along with or believe in someone else's opinions or expertise about how you should heal, you may want to take a moment to tune in to this mantra. Before reciting it, take some time to be alone so that you can find quiet. Perhaps you can get outside in nature or sit in front of a window that has a calming view. Close your eyes and center yourself by placing your feet on the ground. Place your hands in your lap with your fingertips gently touching each other (e.g., prayer hands). Recite this mantra slowly, pause, and then listen to the guidance you receive. If you are still unsure, repeat it daily a few times until you are able to sense and feel your intuition.

My spirit heals me now.

Your spirit is the part of you that has access to special healing abilities. Your spirit is you in your purest form and is infinite in nature. This is different than your soul. Your soul is on a journey and some believe this journey has lasted many lifetimes. Your soul is wise and has the ability to remember what it is like to be connected to your spirit. If you need healing, this mantra encourages you to call on your spirit, giving it permission to reveal more of itself to you.

7

MANTRAS
FOR PROTECTION

"Nothing can dim the light
which shines from within."

Maya Angelou

When you were a child, you learned to protect yourself in many
ways. You were taught to look both ways before crossing a street,
to wear a winter coat before going out in the snow, and to put
sunblock on before going to the beach. Protection mantras are
similar, but they take care of your emotional (energy) body.

You've learned about the energy inside you. There is also
energy outside of you as well. Your physical body has defined
boundaries, but your energy field reaches out much farther. This
field gives you the ability to sense, feel, and pick up on other
people's energy (emotions). Emotions are contagious. If everyone in a room is crying, it will likely have an impact on your
emotions. The various types of energy you pick up depend on
your environment, the types of situations you are in, the people you are around, and the work you do. If the energy around
you is congested and heavy, you may leave the situation feeling

irritated, distracted, exhausted, or frustrated. You may find yourself thinking nonstop about the situation, and have difficulty being in the present moment or feel fearful. These are all signs that you may have absorbed the energy of the environment you were just in.

The mantras in this section are designed to increase your awareness as well as provide you with statements that, when practiced, serve like a protective shield around you. As this occurs, your energy becomes stronger and more resilient. You know this because things will bounce off you more easily. You will feel less bogged down and be able to see clearly the choices that allow you to create a pathway toward inner peace and happiness.

You do it till you don't.

This is another mantra that was ingrained in me by one of my spiritual teachers, Zoe Marae. The words incorporate the power of knowledge, and much of its insight comes from making "mistakes." (Which I don't believe in—they're just choices.) Think of a time when you made the same exact "mistake" (choice) a few times. Perhaps you overreacted about something or neglected to communicate effectively. One of the ways this can happen is when you forget to protect yourself from negativity. For example, you may stifle your breath by overthinking a situation before entering it. Or you may think your boss is going to get annoyed at you for being late to work. Your lack of breathing and overthinking actually set you up for absorbing negativity. You may not realize this is happening until later, when you leave the situation and feel drained or wound up from it. *You do it till you don't* is a mantra that lets you know that sometimes you make the same choices even though they did not work out for you before. This mantra has woken me up on many occasions and made me realize I am the one who has the power to change the pattern.

Feeling is freeing.

You might wonder what this mantra has to do with protection. The answer is *everything*. When you are not feeling, it is likely you are numb or withdrawn. Your lens of consciousness becomes clouded from these types of reactions and you may be less likely to move through situations with awareness and clarity. Breathing is feeling, and feeling is freeing. Be sure to breathe deeply before and after you leave public spaces, your workplace—anywhere you might be susceptible to picking up other people's emotions.

I allow the high-vibrational energy from Mother Earth to support me now. Thank you.

When reciting this mantra, visualize nature. See a large, old tree with its roots system firmly secured into the earth. Remind yourself that the earth is made of high-vibrational energy that is activated by the light brought by the sun and moon. Consider taking time to go outside in your bare feet, touch the center of a flower, or feel the soft drizzle of rain. Nature teaches you what energy feels like when it is flowing and uninterrupted by negativity.

I clear and shield my energy with this beautiful rainbow light.

Rainbows can represent peace, comfort, insight, and life after death. They are one of the few occurrences in life that get you to stop and look up at the sky. Rainbows are also a wonderful way to shield and protect yourself and others from negative influences. Visualize a rainbow light wrapped around you for miles like bubble wrap, keeping you safe and warm. Be sure to add a little extra white, gold, and silver shimmer look to your rainbow. Recite this mantra before bed and it will help you have a good night's sleep.

I am calling forth the highest level of protection now for myself and my family. Thank you.

You cannot protect the people you love by worrying. If anything, worry just contributes to fearful living. Think of protection as activating higher-vibrational energy. Call upon it with your *I am* presence. All you have to do is ask and it will be put into motion. You are a divine being, and because of this your possibilities and capabilities are endless. When you live a life separate from your spirit, you are choosing to be disconnected from who you are. Protect yourself and your loved ones with love and light.

Moving through my feelings brings me joy. I look forward to what is to come.

So many of us have been taught that our emotions are a sign of weakness or a cue that something might be wrong. This could not be further from the truth. Your emotions are the way you are able to connect with yourself and other human beings. These connections represent true strength and are the ultimate form of protection. No one can harm you when you are honest, sincere, and allow yourself to move through (i.e., shed or release) all of your emotions (even the negative ones).

All resistance melts freely from me now.

This mantra relates to the phrase, "What you resist persists." In other words, if you resist feeling free and at ease, your body will learn how to remain in a state of resistance. This is fine if you are truly being threatened, but you are not meant to be in a state of resistance for very long. Resistance holds a congested, heavy energy. As you recite this mantra, see resistance melting, kind of like an ice cream cone on a hot day or a Popsicle in the sun.

I choose to speak up and assert myself now.

Having a strong voice not only protects you but builds confidence. This mantra encourages you to speak up, ask for help, or let people know if something is bothering you. Break any silence and let go of secrets that you have been hiding. Suppressing your thoughts and feelings can lead to high levels of stress, resentment, and dissatisfaction with the ways things are unfolding in your life. It can also live in your body like trauma, holding unpleasant memories in place. Use this mantra as a way to strengthen your voice and build courage.

Moving inward to a place of centeredness strengthens me.

If you are around negativity or feel that someone is taking a lot of energy from you, it's possible that you might react by focusing on an external stressor: a person, situation, phone call, or messy desk. It is kind of like staring at the fuel gauge when your car is running out of gas. As a result, you might get so focused on what you are afraid of that your body starts to go into a fearful state. This mantra reminds you to let go of your external surroundings and instead go inward, where your true strength lies. Tune in to your body, breathe, and focus on your feet, skin, and legs. As you do this, your breath will deepen and you will feel completely protected in love.

I bounce back easily.

It is not uncommon to have days where you feel wiped out or drained. You might have to put extra hours in at work, for example. Or perhaps you had too little sleep due to nursing a new baby. If these draining days persist, you might start thinking that this is a normal way to live. Let me tell you, it is not. This mantra helps you shake off wearying thoughts so that you can get right back on your feet. Be sure to give yourself permission to rest, and also drink plenty of water. Recite this mantra whenever you start to fade or feel run down. Close your eyes, pause, and allow the energy to rest inside of you.

I am light!

The lighter you are, the more aware you become. Emotions such as guilt and shame bog you down, making you feel heavy. Guilt and shame don't stand a chance when you expose them to light. The key is to become aware enough so that you are able to recognize when these emotions are transforming into symptoms such as tightness in your body. This is important because tightness restricts your ability to breathe. Shallow breathing interferes with your ability to truly read and listen to your body's wisdom. See this mantra as a way to invite more light into your body.

My body always has my back.

Part of learning how to protect yourself is learning how to listen to your body's cues. When the hair stands on the back of your neck, or you feel an urge to move away from someone, trust these senses. Likewise, if you're trying to take on too much in your schedule, stop and listen to what is right for your body so as to create balance. This mantra encourages you to trust the little voice inside your heart (not head). Your body has something valuable to tell you. Trust it.

Ha, Ha, Ha, Ha, Ha.

Laughter is truly like medicine. It breaks up negativity, fear, and doubt. The laughing sounds of *ha* and *he* increase the movement of energy in your body. If you feel unprotected and vulnerable to harsh energy, consider watching a funny movie or closing your eyes and thinking of a time when you laughed very hard, deep in your belly. Spend time with people who make you smile and giggle. Laughter is like bug repellent: As soon as fear gets a whiff of it, it flies away.

Calling on Archangel Michael protects me and my loved ones now. Thank you.

I have to admit, I love this guy. Not only is he a spiritual master and an archangel, he is the protector of those who call upon him. He has huge wings and a blue flame sword, and he stands ready to ward off anything that does not serve you. You don't need to be religious to call on him; he is available for all. When you state this mantra, imagine him all around you (above, below, next to). Relax and feel his angelic presence. Avoid feeling like you are asking too much. His job is to protect you. And like most archangels, he respects you enough to wait for you to ask.

I am fearless.

Use this mantra when you find yourself feeling defensive and worried. For example, you might be in a heated conversation with your teenager and nervous about where he is going at night. Rather than project your own fears into the situation, instead choose to center yourself with your breath. If you are really upset, it may help if you put yourself in a tabletop yoga position and breathe. To do this, rest on your hands and knees (wrists below the shoulders). Then fill up your lower abdomen area on inhale, and on exhale tug your navel in. Do this before speaking to your adolescent. (They might think you are crazy, but who cares!) If you don't, you risk feeding the dynamics between you and your teenager with fear. Set boundaries and guidelines from a place of fearlessness with the help of this mantra.

Bathing in your radiant rays now; thank you, sun, for strengthening my aura.

Not only does the sun give you vitamin D, which is essential to maintaining a positive mood and healthy bones, it also strengthens your energy field. Think about how good you feel after sitting (even briefly) in the sun. The sun strengthens the energy field around you (also known as your aura), helping you to become more resilient. If you work or live in a high-pressure or negative environment, consider taking time to go outside for a few minutes a day (particularly if it is sunny). Make this mantra a part of your daily routine.

MANTRAS FOR WEALTH AND PROSPERITY

*"Live life as if everything
were rigged in your favor."*

Rumi

Robert Kiyosaki, the author of *Rich Dad, Poor Dad*, defines the difference between being rich and being wealthy as this: "The rich have lots of money but their bills and finances might keep them up at night; the wealthy, on the other hand, don't worry about money." To be wealthy means you are abundant with resources. Worrying about money depletes energy. Similar to a leaky tire, your fears and concerns may eventually leave you flat. Financial worries tend to be fueled by belief systems of fear and lack. If money is something you are constantly struggling with, this chapter is for you.

It is your reaction to your financial situation that can either empower you or attach you to the very thing you are afraid of. Your finances may not be the actual cause of your blocked feelings about money. When it comes to energy, everything is interconnected. This mean your issues with money could be due to a past or present unresolved relationship with someone. For example, you may feel underpaid and underappreciated by your employer, yet feel you have limited choices. This feeling of being underappreciated may stem from feeling disconnected from yourself—your desires, creativity, and ability to enjoy the moment. It is not a question of whether abundance is there for you, but rather it is a question of your ability to fully open yourself up and receive it. When you are connected to the energy of abundance, you actually don't feel like you are working. Abundance has nothing to do with work; it is an experience based on love, not fear. The mantras in this section take all of this into account.

Before selecting a mantra to work with, let go of how you are expecting the wealth to show up. Sure, we could all use some cash . . . but be open to other avenues. For me, after chanting the Lakshmi chants (in Chapter 11), wealth showed up in the form of a free pile of mulch in my driveway (worth $250!). I support my financial flow by incorporating some of the mantras in this chapter. The key is to relax, have fun, and release the need to control how wealth is revealed to you.

I am limitless.

The first step in moving into your abundant self is letting go of wanting. Every time you want something, you are affirming what you don't have. This mantra reminds you that you are a limitless provider and you have access to unlimited resources. Before anything can happen in the physical, it first needs to be created in the nonphysical (meaning, as energy). As you recite this mantra, see yourself as a limitless form of light. Begin in your wholeness.

I am wealthy.

As you state this mantra, notice what feelings and emotions surface. Very often, people shy away from stating their wealth because they learned to associate wealth with greed, stinginess, and ignorance. They form pictures in their mind of flashy living, insensitive behavior, or people in suits trading stocks. These are beliefs, not truths. Not all wealthy people are inconsiderate or detached from others. This may be a tough pill to swallow. Breathe as you engage with the mantra, release the feelings that show up, and see being wealthy as no different than being worry-free. Having wealth can be very empowering, as it gives you the freedom to support others in many ways.

Now that I am debt–free, having a surplus of energy comes easily.

I have met many clients who want to have more financial flow, yet they live with a debt mindset. This mindset is not exclusive to money. Without awareness, you can have an *I owe you* subconscious belief. For example, if you were a tough child, you might have required a lot of your parents' financial and emotional support. These kinds of experiences can create a belief that you owe your parents for the trouble (energy loss) you caused. Seeing yourself as the cause can lead to self-sabotaging behaviors such as fear of failure or needing to be perfect. As you recite this mantra, give yourself permission to release this self-limiting belief.

Being me is my greatest asset, raising the vibrational flow of everything I do and say.

When it comes to increasing sales and gaining new customers, so many people feel insecure about promoting their ideas, thoughts, feelings, and services. If your energy is weak or doubtful, people will sense this. No matter what aspect of business you want to promote, focus on strengthening your energy first. Slow or inconsistent business may be an indication that your energy is being depleted. Thank the universe for the feedback and recite this mantra whenever uncertain thoughts and feelings appear.

I am open to what the universe has to offer.

You cannot receive what you don't allow. In fact, *allowing* is a prerequisite for *receiving*. In order to become more open to what the universe has to offer, give yourself permission to release any fear of making a mistake. (A mistake is simply a choice!) When you fear making a "mistake," that fear is likely holding you back from trying something new. As you recite this mantra, close your eyes and imagine an open door or window. Allow yourself to feel the energy moving in and out of the opening.

I am choosing to rise!

When it comes to success, there are no accidents. Success is a choice powered by passion, belief, and commitment. The key to success is knowing how to maintain what you create. Many people generate success, but then fear somehow steps in and dismantles it all. This can happen when you start to overextend yourself. For example, you might try to do everything yourself to keep everyone happy, rather than enlist or hire others to support you. Choose to rise by giving yourself permission to take care of yourself no matter what. Let this mantra help you stay focused on what you do best, and allow others to rise in what they do best.

I am blooming.

This mantra was created from the idea that you bloom where you are planted. For example, you may have an idea or expectation in your mind that before you can bloom you have to be in a certain phase of your life, have a particular situation, or have more money. This is a belief, not a truth. You can blossom in any area of your life. Whether you are a mother with small children, exploring a new hobby that brings you joy, or are in the middle of your career blooming, you are thriving and growing through your relationship with energy. By simply choosing to breathe into this moment, you are blooming.

I appreciate all that I am and I live well.

Nothing increases your wealth like gratitude. With gratitude and appreciation, you are likely to experience joy in life. Sure, you see money going out to bills, expenses, and luxuries, but gratitude gives you the ability to trust it will come right back in. Just like the ocean tide and in accordance with the law of harmony, everything will naturally restore and balance itself. Consider creating a gratitude journal that begins each entry with this mantra. Write the mantra out daily, and then underneath it list the things you are grateful for.

Having healed my relationship with money, I am now a money magnet.

Yes, you read this one correctly. Just like you have relationships with other people, you have a relationship with money. This relationship can either be based on fear or love. This mantra is twofold. It heals and attracts at the same time. You don't become a money magnet solely from thinking up the best ideas or having the right connections. Being a money magnet means having heart and soul. It means you believe in your abilities, causes, and services. Be proud of who you are, let go of the past, and keep your head held high as you recite this mantra. See yourself as a money magnet.

Opportunities come my way easily.

If you are concerned that your opportunities are limited—perhaps you have a belief that there are only so many jobs, or that all the good jobs are taken—then this mantra is for you. Be mindful that if you tie up your time and energy with something you don't like, or a job that may be draining you, that choice could interfere with your opportunity to create something new. Recite this mantra daily and avoid choices that don't serve you because you fear you will never have another chance. Opportunities are always available. Allow this mantra to increase your ability to trust this.

I am a leader.

Manifesting money requires leadership. Leaders are known for their resourcefulness. In other words, they are willing to ask for support and hand over a responsibility so that they can focus on what they do best. Leaders also like to inspire and mentor others to develop their own leadership qualities. This is because leaders believe that they have something valuable to share. Before reciting this mantra, take a moment to sit down and reflect on your leadership qualities. Perhaps you are a good listener. Or maybe you are proficient at organizing different phases of a project. Write down four or five qualities and then recite this mantra.

I love making decisions and trust that my instincts serve me well.

Part of living in abundance means learning to love making decisions. This is not to say you won't occasionally go to others for coaching or advice. However, ultimately you are the one who puts these choices into action. The good news is you don't have to make them all with your head. Recite this mantra and then sit and listen to your breathing. Exhale and exhale again. This allows you to drop inside your body for a light meditation (or quiet moment). Instincts might come in a flash. If you are busy thinking and/or rushing around, you can easily miss this flash. As you develop this ability to trust your instincts, making decisions will come with more ease.

I deserve everything I desire.

Since energy cannot be destroyed, neither can your dreams. If you desire a life of abundance—whether it be in health, love, or finances—it is yours if you desire it. The Latin roots of the word *desire* mean "of the father" or "star or heavenly body." Water your desires by reciting this mantra. Know that you are already worthy and enough.

I open the channel to divine abundance.

The channels of abundance exist within your energy centers. One of these centers is at the brow point (in between your eyebrows), which is referred to as your sixth chakra or your third eye. This is the center that activates intuition, giving you access to higher realms. Close your eyes as you recite this mantra and bring your awareness behind your brow. Breathe into this space (inhale through the nose and exhale through the nose) to activate divine abundance.

I am free to produce abundance.

Putting yourself in charge of other people's energy ties you up. It is no different than telling a friend you cannot go out and enjoy a beautiful meal together because you have to work. Being tied up in one area makes it so you can't have experiences in another. Sure, you may have responsibilities and tasks to attend to, but ask yourself how much of your energy is going to managing the experiences of others. For example, think of a mother who chooses not to exercise because she needs to run errands for her children. Or perhaps you are in charge of running an office and find yourself working overtime so that everyone else can take a vacation. This mantra encourages you to release the need to manage others. One way to do this is to listen more without immediately trying to rescue or change the situation. Very often when people have a sounding board, they are able to come up with solutions on their own.

Now that I have released excess fear of being judged, I choose to respect my talents and strengths.

Fear of being judged can hold you back from putting your skills and assets out there for the world to see. Be proud of the skills, knowledge, and experience you have. Don't hesitate to toot your own horn! If you have been working behind the scenes, supporting the success of others, perhaps it is time to make a shift and allow yourself to manifest some of the creative talents and insights you have gathered. Begin the process with this mantra.

I have the confidence and knowledge to take action.

Creating a life of abundance does require some level of action. First, you are going to want to create a plan. Ask yourself, "What steps will I need to take to put things into motion?" After giving it some thought, write down these steps on paper. Be sure to include the resources available to you. Secondly, you will need to cultivate the energy required to put this plan into action. See this mantra as being one of the ways you will create the energy to manifest what you wrote down.

I am resourceful and leverage
my schedule wisely.

Individuals who are manifesting a life of abundance, whether it be in relationships or in finances, often have the ability to manage their time well. If you are looking to strengthen a relationship with your child or partner, consider looking at a way to schedule in time for one another. Do not expect things to fall into place on their own. Be resourceful and leverage your time. For example, if you have to drive your child to a travel soccer game, look into what restaurants are in the area ahead of time. This could prevent you from wasting time later when trying to figure out a place to eat.

9

MANTRAS
FOR PEACE

"Since everything is a reflection
of the mind, everything can
be changed by the mind."

Gautama Buddha

Peace is defined as freedom from disturbance; a sense of calm, tranquility, or serenity. If you were to pull up a picture in your mind of peace, you might imagine a beautiful beach, a mountaintop view, or perhaps a newborn baby sleeping. No doubt peace is something all human beings yearn for. However, without realizing it, you may have some unconscious and conscious ways of going about finding peace—and they may be hindering peace from fully settling into your daily life. For example, you may reserve energy for anticipated problems or people. Perhaps you have someone in your life who requires a lot of your energy or attention. Subconsciously, you may reserve energy (to deal with them later) even when you are not with them. This reservation ultimately disturbs your ability to cultivate and maintain inner peace.

Before you incorporate the following mantras into your life, consider taking a moment to reflect on how you currently refer to peace in your life. For example, I have noticed myself referring to peace in this way: *I just need some peace and quiet, just give me a moment of peace,* or *all I want is peace.* Or maybe you think of peace in less direct ways by noticing bumper stickers and Facebook posts that feature the universal symbol for peace, or words such as *be kind* or *coexist.* Certainly, these symbols and words are proactive ways of promoting peace, but I think it is important to look at the intention behind them. Similar to saying, *I just want some peace,* when it comes to a mantra practice, tone and delivery make a difference in how a message is given and received. Do you tell people to be kind because you think there is a lot of meanness in the world? To create peace, we must get real with ourselves and notice if we are demanding more from others than we are of ourselves. The mantras in this section will assist you.

Seeing is freeing.

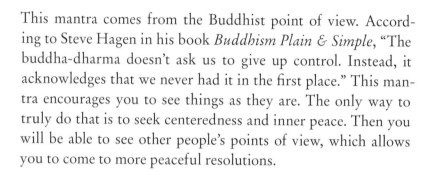

This mantra comes from the Buddhist point of view. According to Steve Hagen in his book *Buddhism Plain & Simple*, "The buddha-dharma doesn't ask us to give up control. Instead, it acknowledges that we never had it in the first place." This mantra encourages you to see things as they are. The only way to truly do that is to seek centeredness and inner peace. Then you will be able to see other people's points of view, which allows you to come to more peaceful resolutions.

I am a river of peace.

Rivers tend to run from higher altitudes to lower altitudes. Gravity causes the water to flow down peaks and valleys, with some water seeping deep into the ground while the remainder rolls off. Being a river of peace is similar. Peace is a higher-vibrational sensation that comes across time and space, trickling down into lower-dimensional frequencies such as the human body. As you recite this mantra, connect to it visually while closing your eyes.

Let it be.

The mantra *Let it be* comes from the famous Beatles' song "Let It Be." Sometimes the best response to "times of trouble" is to do nothing and to let things rest and be as they are. When you find yourself attempting to control an outcome or are disappointed by the results of an effort, state this mantra. Embrace it as a source of comfort and strength.

Be here, right now.

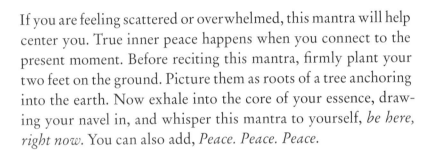

If you are feeling scattered or overwhelmed, this mantra will help center you. True inner peace happens when you connect to the present moment. Before reciting this mantra, firmly plant your two feet on the ground. Picture them as roots of a tree anchoring into the earth. Now exhale into the core of your essence, drawing your navel in, and whisper this mantra to yourself, *be here, right now.* You can also add, *Peace. Peace. Peace.*

Metta.

Metta is a Pali (early language of Buddhism) word that has a variety of meanings, some of which include: love, peace, nonviolence, goodwill, generosity, and more. You can also find the word *metta* used in the healing community, as it refers to a loving-kindness practice. Notice how when you repeat it your tongue taps the roof of your mouth. Visualize beautiful colors when you recite this mantra. See your words as a powerful vibration pulsating into the atmosphere.

I am whole.

Choose this mantra when you feel you are overfocusing on what isn't working. For example, if you find yourself focusing on lack (e.g., what you don't have or what is missing in your life), remember you are a soul first. You come from infinite light and spaciousness. If your mindset is focused on lack, it is just a sign that you have separated from who you are. Allow this mantra to bring you back into your wholeness. Visualize the universe and its spaciousness as you recite it.

I already have everything I need.

Putting timelines in your life may help you stay on task. However, if you find you are feeling pressured by having to achieve something in a certain order or by a certain deadline, consider reciting this mantra. Your accomplishments may very well be something to strive for, but they by no means measure your worth. This mantra reminds you that you already have everything you need. Setting goals and pursuing your dreams expand who you already are rather than who you hope or wish to be.

I honor these sensations fully, and by doing so I honor the love we share.

Deep loss and sadness can make peace seem far-fetched and elusive. Grief is a natural and necessary part of the human experience. However, in order for grief to serve you, you must honor its presence. Take time to sit with your emotions, feel them, and give them permission to pass through you. Rituals such as lighting a candle or saying a prayer can assist you with this process. Know you are not alone.

My heart is beating with peace and love.

When reciting this mantra, imagine a beautiful pink light around your heart center. Allow this light to rest there while you breathe in and out. Feel the light as it sits on the front and back of your heart space, similar to how you might shine a flashlight. As you breathe, imagine this light growing stronger, radiating out in front of you, behind you, and alongside of you. Repeat this mantra, *My heart is beating with peace and love.* Imagine this mantra running through all chambers of your heart, creating an inner glow deep inside you.

Breathing space.

After reciting this mantra, ask yourself some important questions. Where is my breathing space? Where do I feel most at ease? What time of day is most peaceful to me? Consider taking a moment to roam outside. Be curious about the breathing spaces around you. Perhaps you'll notice a tree, your front porch step, or a certain pathway. A breathing space can also be a special area in your home where you limit distractions (such as a television and/or a computer). Such a space might be a certain chair or spot at the kitchen table where you see the birds clearly through a window.

Merciful me.

If you feel impatient or easily annoyed by someone or something, recite this mantra. It calls on the aspect of you that is forgiving, flexible, and willing to back off. Whisper these words as if you are speaking to your heart. The heart area is where you can hold and, in some cases, wrestle with old energy. Without tools (such as mantras) and awareness to help you let go of this old energy, you might experience an increase in tension and irritability. Take a deep inhale (inflate the belly), and then on exhale whisper these words until you are all out of breath. Extend the exhale by pulling in your navel when you are done.

I believe in faith.

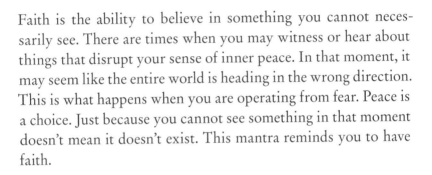

Faith is the ability to believe in something you cannot necessarily see. There are times when you may witness or hear about things that disrupt your sense of inner peace. In that moment, it may seem like the entire world is heading in the wrong direction. This is what happens when you are operating from fear. Peace is a choice. Just because you cannot see something in that moment doesn't mean it doesn't exist. This mantra reminds you to have faith.

(Inhale, exhale)
This is my peace practice.

A practice is something you choose to repeat daily. Think about it: If you wanted to get good at playing the piano, then you would most likely practice it on a daily basis. The same goes for writing, reading, or playing a sport. Developing peace in your daily life is no different. The more you practice breathing, the better you get at it. Only instead of learning how to breathe faster, you will breathe deeply and slowly with conscious awareness.

Peace echos through me now.

Nature is filled with sounds of peace. The sound of water trickling outside of your window, birds chirping, or the breeze blowing gently through the trees can soothe your nervous system. Take time to listen and notice these sounds in your daily life. If these sounds get disrupted, as they sometimes do (e.g., leaf blowers, children crying), learn to develop your ability to notice what is near and far. Sure the leaf blower might be loud and disruptive, but remember the closest sound you have is the sound of your breath. Withdraw (e.g., close the window) from distractions the best you can and return to your breath.

Neutralizing drama now.

Drama is created from conflict, insecurity, and pain. Perhaps you live in a family where gossip and conflict are common. Or maybe your workplace environment is like this. These types of family and/or work dynamics can get quite heated with tension. In an attempt to cope with the situation, you may be forced to detach yourself from it all. This may work to some degree, but tuning out or walking away is only a part of the process. See yourself as becoming neutral to what is happening. This means the drama does not impact you either way. In other words, you are able to observe without being drawn in.

I am soulful and serve with compassion.

To be compassionate means to love others as you love yourself. Empathy, on the other hand, is when you are able to see the world through someone else's viewpoint. Without awareness, empathy can actually disturb your sense of inner peace. This is because you may have learned (unconsciously) to take on the emotions (the fears and anxieties) of others as you were attempting to understand their viewpoint. When you engage in life from your soul, you are able to see that everyone is capable, and therefore you resist the urge to take on their worries and problems. They can handle them on their own. Utilize this mantra to remind you of who you are and how your soulfulness serves.

My breath is deep;
my eyes are soft;
I am at peace.

You are taught many things as a child: how to tie your shoes, brush your teeth, and read and write. Breathing is not something most people were taught how to do. As the benefits of mindfulness (and mantras) spread, this fortunately is beginning to shift. You do not have to be formally trained to learn how to breathe well. You can start right now by reciting this mantra. Take a long, slow, deep inhale (inflating your lower belly) and a slow, extended exhale (drawing your navel in), reciting this mantra in between. Do this for five rounds.

I release all surplus fear of relapse.
I can handle anything now.

When people find peace, something interesting can happen. Individuals who have a history of anxiety may start to worry that something bad is going to take away their newfound peace. This happens particularly with individuals who have been through a recovery program—they do great at first, but then start to slip. This mantra encourages you to release all fears of relapse. With that said, know it is perfectly normal to have off days, so long as you get back on your feet again.

10

MANTRAS FOR NEW BEGINNINGS

"Whether you believe you can
do a thing or not, you are right."

Henry Ford

Each New Year, millions of people around the world uphold the tradition of creating New Year's resolutions. This is a time when we commit to acts of self-improvement for ourselves and the greater good of others. But, according to the Statistic Brain Research Institute, of the 45 percent of Americans who actually make a resolution, only a meager 8 percent will actually keep them. The truth is, you do not have to wait until a new year to begin again. In fact, each day gives you an opportunity to start fresh. Rather than resort to old ways of going about this, allow mantras to support you in your efforts to clean your slate.

You may be wondering why resolutions fail and how mantras can help. Psychology professor Peter Herman and his colleagues point to what they call "false hope syndrome." People really want to change, but in addition to making their goals unrealistic, they often put into motion affirmations they really don't believe.

Since mantras tend to be more energy-focused, they can help you shift internally by aligning your energetic vibration with the very thing you choose to manifest in your life. This is not to say affirmations are not a beautiful tool for maintaining this energy, but initially it is best to engage in a true mantra practice. Here is how it works. Because of their repetition and meditative qualities, mantras encourage your attention to focus on the practice rather than the words themselves. In this section, you will be guided through a variety of mantras that speak to some of life's natural transitions. I strongly suggest you repeat these mantras mindfully, observing how they feel in your body—the vibrations they carry as well as the sensations they may stir up. Know they are preparing your body's energy for the integration of this new way of being. Pick one or two and stick with them for at least thirty days, following the insight and guidelines provided.

I welcome the gift of this day.

One thing you can count on is that the sun will rise and you will have a chance to begin again. Seeing each day as a gift is one way to begin again. When you attach past events to present situations, life can feel like a struggle. This mindset can foster beliefs such as *My life has always been hard*, giving you the impression that life is a burden. You get to have another chance given to you for free. Take it and accept this day as a gift.

I am evolving and changing for the better.

This mantra reminds you that because you are made of energy, you are always in motion. We know cells have the ability to regenerate themselves. Since you are made of trillions of cells, you are never exactly the same as you were the day before. See change as part of your evolution. Using this mantra is a positive way to support the evolution of your brain, mind, body, and spirit.

Uncertainty awakens me now.
I trust this path.

There is no right or wrong path. All paths lead to the heart. Live in love and your path will be illuminated for you. Like most paths, don't be surprised if there are twists and turns. Stay focused on the moment. State this mantra when you start to second-guess your decisions or question your capabilities. It is not that you won't change your mind from time to time, but let this be part of the eternal flow of life.

Everything happens for me.

Have you had a time when you thought you were going in one direction and then found yourself moving in another? Perhaps you started in one school but found yourself transferring to another. Or maybe you were certain you found your life partner, but then had a change of heart. This mantra is for those times. You are always being guided. Resist the urge to compare or measure your path against the paths of others. Believe everything has a greater purpose.

I am enough.

Very often, new beginnings can be looked at like a game of Monopoly—one wrong move and you are forced to go back to the start. For example, you might start a new business and then suddenly fear you don't have enough experience. Or maybe you are a new mother and suddenly feel overwhelmed by the responsibility. Take a moment and breathe in through your nose and out through your mouth. Slow down. Connect to your heart and state this mantra out loud.

These sensations sweep through me swiftly now. Thank you.

New beginnings are often accompanied by expectations and pressure. These perceptions drain your energy, giving you the impression that new beginnings are full of hardship and struggle. Many people may be cheering you on, while you are your greatest critic. This may be because you have bought into the mindset that things have to be difficult; otherwise it is a sign you are not working hard enough. This brings about expectations of strain. For example, if you are starting a new school, are you expecting the classes to be so difficult that you will have no time for yourself? If you are starting a business venture, have you set yourself up for burnout? Be sure to breathe and really sink into the feeling behind this mantra. See your body as a filter that sifts out all impure thoughts and beliefs.

It is my free will to put my awareness and attention into the infinite source of energy I am. I am trust, I love, and I am free.

If you feel other people or situations are in charge of your course, this mantra is for you. I have met many people who have given up their power. Ask yourself three questions now. How do you know when you are in your power? Do you rely on feedback from others? Is there something you long for or believe you need in order to achieve your goals? Think of your free will as a pool of water. The more attention and energy you put into needing to have other people's approval or feedback, the bigger that pool gets. Your free will is infinite; it has no end. It runs wide and deep. It is vast and strong. You can choose which areas of your life you would like to deepen. Wherever you put your attention energy will pool. I say put the attention back on yourself and shift this pattern by reciting this mantra in a strong, clear voice several times a day. Exhale at the end of your statement.

I am taking the time to savor and relish the food that nourishes me now. Thank you.

The number one New Year's resolution for Americans is wanting to lose weight. If this is your resolution, then know that it comes with an opportunity to change and heal your relationship with food. Be mindful of both how you look at (or judge) what you eat and the words you use to describe your food. For example, thinking of food as being good or bad, junk or healthy, may not serve you as well as you like. Think about it. What happens when you allow yourself to actually partake in what you call "junk" food? It is likely to make you feel lousy, incapable, and in many cases like a failure. Rather than compare and contrast food, put your attention on this mantra. Eating is not a time for criticism; it is a time for gratitude, nourishment, and (let's face it) pleasure. This mantra encourages you to slow down, breathe, check in, and be present to your choices.

I say yes to daily activity.

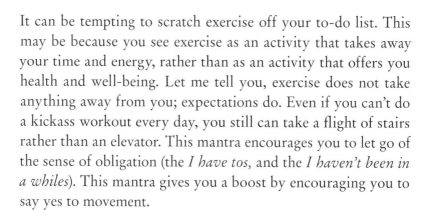

It can be tempting to scratch exercise off your to-do list. This may be because you see exercise as an activity that takes away your time and energy, rather than as an activity that offers you health and well-being. Let me tell you, exercise does not take anything away from you; expectations do. Even if you can't do a kickass workout every day, you still can take a flight of stairs rather than an elevator. This mantra encourages you to let go of the sense of obligation (the *I have tos,* and the *I haven't been in a whiles*). This mantra gives you a boost by encouraging you to say yes to movement.

I am the light of perfection.

My baby is the light of perfection.

Our family is the light of perfection now.

Your parenting journey will be anything but perfect. In fact, you will be on a journey that is often marked by imperfections. Everything you once knew changes. Suddenly, that nice clean white shirt you have worn for years doesn't quite fit the same, and it also has spit-up stains on it. Outward appearances are not the only thing that changes. Finances, schedules, and your sex life also become upended. Let go of attempting to hold on to what once was. This mantra encourages you to replace perfection with presence. Put your attention on your light and know you are on a well-traveled journey.

Life happens for me. I am always being guided and supported.

Sometimes new beginnings come on without warning. Some examples are a sudden loss of a job, a change in a living situation, or an unexpected breakup. If you take the time to reflect on the challenges, you often can see that they were some of your greatest moments of growth. This mantra reminds you that life doesn't happen *to* you; it happens *for* you. You are always being guided and supported.

I allow this purification to take place through me now, strengthening my "I am" presence.

New beginnings are an opportunity to clean up and clear out your surroundings. Something as simple as cleaning out a sock drawer, purging your closet, or changing the positioning of your furniture can make a world of difference. Clutter actually congests energy. Notice the spaces and places in your environment that could use a spring cleaning, no matter what time of year it is. Break down the tasks into manageable steps, perhaps a couple of drawers a day. Don't be afraid to throw some things out or donate them. You would be surprised to see how much energy you can gain from it. Allow this mantra to support you through the process.

Choice is freedom.

I choose to _____.

●●

Feeling stuck means you believe you have limited choices. Listen to the words you use to describe your situation. If you hear yourself saying statements such as, "I have to" or "I should," then it is likely you are feeling powerless. Use this mantra to help you to move whatever obstacle you believe is in your way. It gets you to fill in the blank with an empowering statement. For example, rather than saying, "I have to go to work," instead say, "I choose to go to work." This phrasing gives you more energy and puts you back in the driver's seat as a cocreator of your life experiences.

Having this opportunity brings me closer to my aspirations now. I am grateful.

A career and job are not the same. A job is something you do to make money to prepare, or support, you on a path toward your career. Some jobs evolve into careers. It is not uncommon to have a few jobs before settling into a career commitment. The point being, jobs—even if they are not related to your aspirations—often are the seeds and early plantings for forming your career. They teach you valuable skills that are likely to come in handy later.

I enjoy learning and take full ownership of my education.

Attending a new school is a big deal at any stage in life. This mantra encourages you to take full ownership of your choices, even if you still have some reservations about going. Having one foot in the door and one foot out will only confuse your energy. Recite this mantra as a way to be committed to this opportunity. Be sure to help this mantra come to fruition through you by breathing into it, similar to blowing a bubble. Otherwise, the words may fall flat. Allow yourself to transition to a place of wholeness in mind, body, and spirit. Empower the process by being proactive about your schedule, teachers, and choices.

Love and light pour into every space in this home now.

Before you fill a space with things such as furniture and personal items, recite a mantra as a way to bless your home. This is different than a religious blessing, which is typically done by a reverend or priest. Give yourself a moment to sit in each room. Close your eyes and visualize white light pouring into the space. You can also recite this mantra after you have moved in. Follow the same instructions, and set your intention by bringing yourself to the present moment before reciting.

Feelings change; God and love are infinite.

Love is always present even when you can't feel it. This is because love is a high-vibrational energy that connects you to your spirit. Marriage can be wonderful and exciting. When you live in close proximity with someone (sharing goals, hardships, and dreams), you can, over time, become sensitive to that other person's energy. For example, if your partner is having a bad day, without realizing it, you can begin to feel crummy as well. This mantra gives you a way to honor your marriage and feel supported by your faith.

Through my "I am" presence, I allow and bless the completion of this marriage. May all surplus anger, resentment, and disappointment be recycled into unconditional love, and so be it.

Marriages don't come to an end; they come to completion. Underneath it all, most marriages are sacred contracts that some believe were made before we came to be on this earth. Not all marriages are completed by mutual agreement. Regardless, it can be heartbreaking and sad when partnerships move in separate directions. Even though you physically and financially may move on, hurtful emotions can linger, leading to ambivalence and distrust. Allow this mantra to support your healing so that you can open your heart and begin again.

11

SACRED MANTRAS

"Mantras are passwords
that transform the mundane
into the sacred."

Deva Premal

The mantras in this section have been preserved for thousands of years. As discussed in Chapter 1, they are based on seed sounds. Each seed sound corresponds to one of your energy centers (chakras). Similar to the variations found in languages, there are multiple variations of seed sounds. The ones I suggest getting to know before moving on in this section are: Lam, Vam, Ram, Yam, Ham, and Om (Aum). Beginning with the base of your spine, these sounds travel up your body to the crown of your head. Lam begins at the base (pelvis area), Vam is underneath your navel, Ram is in your mid-section, Yam is around your heart center, Ham is in the throat/chest area, and Om is in the space between your eyebrows.

Think of these sounds as an introduction to the mantras noted in this chapter. Similar to fine-tuning an instrument, seed sounds fine-tune your awareness to the sacred vibration that mantras offer. State them out loud three times in a row (Lam, Vam, Ram, Yam, Ham, Om), pause, and allow yourself to feel the sensations. These sensations are a signal that your body is tuning itself into this higher vibration. You are likely to notice some inner movement right away. You can continue with this daily attunement while incorporating some of the mantras that follow.

Browse through the list and select one to work with for forty days. If at any point you feel out of sorts, feel free to take a day or two off. Think of sacred mantras as similar to a fire. Each time you chant a round (108 times), you are throwing a log on the fire. If the fire gets too big, you can choose to take a break and let it burn on its own for a bit.

Finally, when chanting mantras, you do not need to be in charge. In other words, you do not direct the experience; your body does. Your body will take in what it needs and adjust itself accordingly. Allow yourself to trust, feel, and be grateful for the experience.

Lokah Samastah Sukhino Bhavantu

PRONUNCIATION: low-kaah'-ha suh-mu-staah'-ha soo-khee-no' bu-uh-vun-too

TRANSLATION: "May all beings everywhere be happy and free, and may the thoughts, words, and actions of my own life contribute in some way to that happiness and to that freedom for all."

Translated by Sharon Gannon, cofounder of Jivamukti Yoga

This mantra reminds us that no one is really free from suffering entirely until we are *all* free. This is a beautiful chant to teach children or to utilize yourself as a means for increasing happiness worldwide. In light of some of the terror we and our children have been exposed to, whether it is through media or an actual incident, this chant gives us a tangible tool for moving through the overwhelming feelings these images and experiences bring. Remember, fear cannot survive in love. They cannot both exist.

Om Ram Ramaya Namaha

PRONUNCIATION: aum rahm rahm-eye-yah nahm-ah-hah

TRANSLATION: I offer these words to Rama, whose perfection exists in us all.

This mantra calls to awaken and balance dormant energy within the solar plexus area (navel) as well as balances out the energy down the right and left sides of the body. *Ram* in Sanskrit is the seed sound for the navel area (manipura chakra); it can be translated as the one that gives happiness (God-like). This mantra is especially helpful if you are someone who suffers from anxiety and depression. It is known to balance out the nervous system. As for the word *Rama*, according to *Healing Mantras*, *Ra* runs down the right side of the body (solar current) and *ma* (lunar current) runs down the left. Each current crisscrosses at the center. If you are feeling overwhelmed or have a habit of turning to your thoughts as a way to problem solve, fix, or control what is happening, this mantra may be a good fit for your daily practice.

If you are over the age of twenty-five, change the ending of this mantra from *Namaha* to *Swaha*, as the energies in the body change after age twenty-five.

Om Klim Kalika-Yei Namaha

PRONUNCIATION: aum kleem kah-lee-kah-yea nahm-ah-hah

TRANSLATION: "I salute Kali and ask her to bring balance and alignment to a situation or relationship quickly."

From *Shakti Mantras*

The ego lives off fear, not love. It is the part of you that questions, doubts, and worries. This suppresses your connection to love. This mantra calls on the Hindu goddess Kali. Kali is known to be fierce, fighting off any evil. This Hindu goddess is called upon for her powerful abilities to both protect you from negativity and release you from the reins of ego.

Notice this mantra includes the seed sounds of Om and Klim (Kleem). Chanted alone, Kleem is a mantra for spiritual development. It stimulates the lower half of your body, helping you to feel more centered, calm, and creative. Engage this chant when you find yourself attaching to negative thinking or when you need things to look a certain way before you can accept them. This is all ego-based thinking, and as you surrender your ego, your spiritual journey will deepen.

Om Tare Tuttare Ture Swaha

PRONUNCIATION: aum tah-rei too-tah-rei too-rei swah-hah

TRANSLATION: "Om and salutations to She (Tara), who is the source of all blessings."

From *Shakti Mantras*

In Hinduism and Tibetan Buddhism, Tara is known as the divine mother. The White Tara, which is what this mantra is referring to, is often referred to as the mother of Buddha. The White Tara can be called on for protection and great compassion, two qualities that make her very powerful. There are other aspects of Tara that have been manifested through other colors such as Green Tara, Pink Tara, and Light Brown Tara. I include the White Tara because she is a great place to start. I have found that she undeniably provides quick removal of and protection from negative energy. Call on her when you want to clear a space, such as your work or home environment, of heavy, negative energy.

He Ma Durga

PRONUNCIATION: hey ma durga

TRANSLATION: "I bow down again and again to the Goddess who is manifest in all creatures as strength and power."

From BhaktiBreakfastClub.com

He is similar to saying "Oh" in the English language. *Ma* in Sanskrit means mother. *Durga* can be thought of as transformative energy (goddess). This mantra refers to the divine feminine energy (e.g., Mother Mary). It is chanted as a way to release parts of your personality that no longer serve you, including impatience, self-criticism, judgement, and jealousy. Chant this mantra as a conscious way to release parts of your personality that may be interfering with your ability to see truth and be connected to the divine being that you are. Yes, your personality can be changed—nothing is fixed unless you allow it to be.

Om Gam Ganapataye Namaha

PRONUNCIATION: aum gum gah-nah-paht-ah-yeh nahm-ah-hah

TRANSLATION: Wake up the energy located in the root chakra (pelvic floor region) and remove all obstacles, tapping into the powerful energy of Ganesh.

Ganesh is one of the most worshipped Hindu gods. He is often prayed and chanted to, particularly when people are beginning a new business or adventure. Ganesh is often represented as an elephant head on a human body. He is known as the lord of good fortune, as he will help you remove all obstacles. He destroys all pride, vanity, and selfishness. With that said, in the Hindu culture, Ganesh is a symbol of abundance and will support you in reaching your ideal goal. Chant this mantra when you are beginning something new, and have no doubts that Ganesh will be there supporting you in that venture.

11. Sacred Mantras

Har Har Mukanday

PRONUNCIATION: har har moo-kan-day

TRANSLATION: The infinite creator liberates me.

Har comes from the word *Hari*, which means God. *Mukanday* means liberating aspects of yourself. One of the best ways to experience this mantra is through music. Various artists such as Mirabai Ceiba offer such music (available on iTunes). It is a very soothing mantra. When you recite it, you are asking the creator to release you of anything you no longer need. As you recite it, trust that your creator (God, or whomever you identify with) knows what would be in your best interest to release.

Om Hrim Taha

PRONUNCIATION: aum hreem ta-ha

TRANSLATION: I cancel this heat (anger) in me through the energy of light.

Anger can have many different expressions. Some people use the word *frustration* to describe their anger because frustration is a more socially accepted emotion. When it comes to this mantra, it does not matter whether you tend to run on a short fuse, hold in your anger, or express your anger in more passive-aggressive ways (e.g., saying, "I'm fine"). As you recite it, trust that your body will take in and adjust itself according to your needs. What you can do, however, is center yourself through breathing and, if you like, add a visualization.

In this case imagine yourself pushing the Cancel or Delete button on your computer, or turning off the heat on your stove. The sounds in this chant bring that heat right down so you can think clearly and act appropriately. I suggest you chant this mantra when you are not angry so that you can memorize it. Then when you get heated up you will be more likely to utilize it as a resource.

Om Shanti

PRONUNCIATION: aum shh-aunt-eee

TRANSLATION: Infinite consciousness for peace, calm, and bliss for everyone everywhere.

The word *shanti* can mean peace, bliss, and calm for everyone in every way. Tradition recommends that this Hindu chant be repeated a minimum of three times. One for the body, one for speech, and one for the mind. This chant removes anything interfering with peace. Use it to cleanse the words that come out of your mouth. You can also chant *Om Shanti* before sending an e-mail, making a phone call, walking into a store, or tending to a task. See it as removing anything that might disturb peaceful interactions.

Sa Ta Na Ma

PRONUNCIATION: saa taa naa maa

TRANSLATION: The complete cycle beginning with the universe transforming into life, death, and rebirth.

This mantra has the power to break the habit of addiction. It actually rearranges your subconscious mind, removing beliefs and emotions that feed these impulses and urges. According to author Ramdesh Kaur, "Sa Ta Na Ma helps to regulate and soothe your mind, relaxing it and syncing it back up." This mantra is also great for increasing intuition and stimulating change.

Snatam Kaur, a spiritual musician known as the voice of an angel, chants a beautiful version of this mantra. Her music can be found on iTunes and YouTube.

Shreem

PRONUNCIATION: shh-reem

TRANSLATION: "Shreem is a special seed sound indicating creativity, blessings, grace, surrender, and peace. It reflects the energy of the moon, the feminine nature, receptivity, and the power of Lakshmi, the force of Divine abundance and prosperity."

From the Chopra Center

This mantra is the seed sound for abundance. It is related to the Hindu goddess Lakshmi. *Shreem* almost sounds similar to *stream*, meaning flow of abundance. Lakshmi is the Hindu goddess of wealth and fortune both material and physical.

Since this mantra is one word, it is quite easy to incorporate into daily living. I find myself chanting it while I am driving or when I start to focus on lack. Notice how you interact with abundance. How do you respond when you see a nice car or a family with lots of children? These kinds of daily experiences often reflect abundance blocks. Take note without judgment. Breathe and chant *shreem* to help you overcome these fears and anxieties.

Om Mani Padme Hum

PRONUNCIATION: aum ma-nee pod-may hum

TRANSLATION: May these obstacles be cleared at the source of creation, bringing me in alignment with my divine self.

Oh, how I love this mantra! It is multifaceted. This mantra is about clearing obstacles and evoking compassion. I had been chanting this mantra for about thirty days (108 times a day) when the opportunity to write this book came my way.

Clearing obstacles is one thing, but doing it with compassion is another. And that is why it may come as no surprise that this chant is also associated with Kwan Yin, the goddess of compassion. Kwan Yin reminds us to reflect without judgement. This mantra will help you honor all changes with respect, love, and kindness.

Aham Prema

PRONUNCIATION: ah-hum pray-ma

TRANSLATION: I am divine love.

This mantra evokes the divine love in you. But to truly fall in love, you must first learn how to love and respect yourself. Before writing down or visualizing the ideal partner you would like to bring into your life, consider chanting this mantra over a forty-day period. Get to know yourself as divine love and light. Allow the chant to transform any beliefs, emotions, or events that have distracted or buried the memory of you as love. You may feel you have to find love, but this chant reminds you that you are already all of that and more. As you chant this, visualize beautiful colors of green, pinks, and reds around your heart center.

Om Sri Rama Jaya Rama Jaya Jaya Rama

PRONUNCIATION: aum shree rah-mah jah-yah rah-mah jah-yah jah-yah rah-mah

TRANSLATION: "Om and Victory to Rama (the self within), victory, victory to Rama."

From SanskritMantra.com

It has been reported that Mahatma Gandhi practiced this mantra for more than sixty years, originally being introduced to it by his nurse when he was a small boy. It is no wonder he led his country of India to independence through a peaceful movement of nonviolent approaches. *Om* is the seed sound for universal consciousness, *sri* is a mantra that salutes and activates feminine power, *rama* refers to the divine self in all of us, and *jaya* means victory.

Om Namah Shivaya

PRONUNCIATION: aum nah-mah shee-vah-yah

TRANSLATION: "Om and salutations to that which I am capable of becoming."

From SanskritMantra.com

This mantra is great for many things, and one of them is healing misunderstandings in relationships. According to *Healing Mantras*, when chanting this mantra know that you are asking to clear up any confusion so as to gain strength and focus on good intentions. The two syllables *na* and *ma* can be translated as, "I humbly bow to you." The three syllables *shi-va-ya* invoke Lord Shiva. Lord Shiva, one of the most powerful and complex gods in the Hindu culture, is known for his teachings on self-control and discipline. Certainly, these qualities are essential when learning to resolve conflicts and misunderstandings peacefully.

Om Sri Dhanvantre Namaha

PRONUNCIATION: aum shree don-von-threy nahm-ah-hah

TRANSLATION: Salutations to the divine healer.

This chant is a request to strengthen your healing abilities mentally, physically, and emotionally. Perhaps this is why *Healing Mantras* reported, "In traditional households in southern India, women chant this mantra as they prepare food to infuse it with the powerful healing vibrations that ward off disease." Consider placing your hands over the food you are about to serve and reciting this mantra. State it one time and then pause and hold your hands steady over the food for a few seconds. If you are caring for someone who is sick, you might want to do a full 108 chants a day to strengthen your abilities to support their healing. This is a great mantra for nurses, doctors, and healers.

Sat Nam

PRONUNCIATION: Sa T Nam

TRANSLATION: Truth is in my name. Truth is my identity.

When moving through your daily routines and schedules, it can be easy to begin to identify with the roles your tasks require. Perhaps you see yourself primarily as a mother, son, daughter, father, student, provider, friend, boss, or employee. Or perhaps you see the labels that may have been used to describe you. For example, if you have been diagnosed with a health condition (anxiety, attention deficit disorder, or some other type of health challenge), you might label yourself with it. Maybe you believe people see you as lazy, overprotective, or stubborn. These types of identities can obstruct you from seeing the truth of who you are; your true identity. This mantra removes the layers (labels) of illusion, bringing you to the truth of who you are. You are a creator, you are energy, and you are free.

Om Sri Maha Lakshmiyei Swaha

PRONUNCIATION: aum shree mah-ha laksh-mee-yei swah-ha

TRANSLATION: "Om and salutations. I invoke the Great Feminine Principal of Abundance."

From *Healing Mantras*

I first was introduced to Goddess Lakshmi at a craft fair when I purchased a necklace with her image on it. Little did I know at the time how powerful she is. Today, I refer to her as my best friend. Lakshmi is the great goddess of wealth and prosperity. She brings good fortune to all who commit to a practice of chanting to her for a minimum of forty days. Know when you recite this mantra, you are calling on the abundance of everything: health, finances, friendships, love, food, etc. You do not need to focus on yourself when reciting it. You are calling the presence of this higher energy and allowing it to spill over into the lives of others. If you are age twenty-five or under, end this chant with *Namaha* rather than *Swaha*.

BIBLIOGRAPHY

Adiswarananda, Swami. *Meditation & Its Practices.* SkyLight Paths. Woodstock, VT. 2003. Pp. 95, 128.

Ashley-Farrand, Thomas. *Chakra Mantras.* Weiser Books. San Francisco, CA. 2006. P. 158.

Ashley-Farrand, Thomas. *Healing Mantras.* Ballantine Wellspring. New York, NY. 1999. Pp. 48, 112, 121, 143, 151, 208.

Ashley-Farrand, Thomas. *Shakti Mantras.* Ballantine Books. New York, NY. 2003. P. 137.

Atkins, Charles. *Modern Buddhist Healing.* Nicolas-Hays. York Beach, ME. 2002. Pp. 10, 38.

Bhajan, Yogi. "Science of Mantra Meditation." HariSingh.com. www.harisingh.com/ScienceOfMantra.htm.

Chopra, Deepak. "What Is Primordial Sound Meditation?" The Chopra Center. www.chopra.com/ccl/what-is-primordial-sound-meditation.

Dweck, Dr. Carol. *Mindset Works.* "The Science." www.mindsetworks.com/webnav/whatismindset.aspx.

Feuerstein, Georg. "200 Key Sanskrit Yoga Terms." "Prasada." *Yoga Journal.* August 28, 2007. www.yogajournal.com/article/beginners/200-key-sanskrit-yoga-terms.

Fosar, Grazyna, and Franz Bludorf. "Scientists Prove DNA Can Be Reprogrammed by Words and Frequencies."

Wake Up World. http://wakeup-world.com/2011/07/12/ scientist-prove-dna-can-be-reprogrammed-by-words-frequencies.

Gallo, Andrea. Gayatri Mantra . . . The Essence Of All Mantras. www.mestizamalas.com/#!mantras/cbe2.

Gannon, Sharon. *Insight State*. "Lokah Samastah Sukhino Bhavantu— May All Beings Be Happy and Free." www.insightstate.com/video/ lokah-samastah-sukhino-bhavantu.

Hagen, Steve. *Buddhism Plain & Simple*. Broadway Books. New York, NY. 1997. P. 51.

Happify Daily. "The 5 Skills That Will Increase Your Happiness." http:// my.happify.com/hd/the-5-skills-that-will-increase-your-happiness.

Kaur, Ramdesh. "3 Mantras to Help Insomnia." *Spirit Voyage*. May 22, 2012. www.spiritvoyage.com/blog/index.php/3-mantras-to-help-insomnia.

Kiyosaki, Robert. "The Definition of Wealth." *Rich Dad*. May 28, 2013. www.richdad.com/Resources/Rich-Dad-Financial-Education-Blog/May-2013/the-definition-of-wealth.aspx.

Konrath, Sara. "How Volunteering Can Lessen Depression and Extend Your Life." *Everyday Health*. www.everydayhealth.com/ depression/how-volunteering-can-lessen-depression-and-extend-your-life.aspx.

Mall, Sarin. "How to Change Body Forms by Chanting AUM or Mantra." Mallstuffs.com. March 20, 2014. www.mallstuffs.com/Blogs/ BlogDetails.aspx?BlogId=375&BlogType=Spiritual&Topic=How%20 to%20change%20body%20forms%20by%20chanting%20AUM%20 or%20mantra.

Marae, Zoe. https://zoeography.myshopify.com.

McGonigal, Kelly. *The Upside of Stress*. Penguin Publishing Group. New York, NY. 2015.

McQuaid, Michelle. "Ten Reasons to Focus on Your Strengths." *Psychology Today*. November 11, 2014. www.psychologytoday.com/blog/functioning-flourishing/201411/ten-reasons-focus-your-strengths.

Murphy, Brendan D. "Junk DNA: Our Interdimensional Doorway to Transformation." *World Mysteries*. September 8, 2014. http://blog.world-mysteries.com/science/junk-dna-our-interdimensional-doorway-to-transformation.

Price-Mitchell, Marilyn. "Does Nature Make Us Happy?" *Psychology Today*. March 27, 2014. www.psychologytoday.com/blog/the-moment-youth/201403/does-nature-make-us-happy.

Rajhans, Gyan. "The Power of Mantra Chanting." About.com. http://hinduism.about.com/od/prayersmantras/a/mantrachanting.htm.

Ram, Dass, with Rameshwar Das. *Polishing the Mirror: How to Live from Your Spiritual Heart*. Sounds True. Boulder, CO. 2013. P. 3

Rankin, Lissa, MD. *Mind Over Medicine*. Hay House. New York, NY. 2013. Pp. 8, 147.

Rinchen, Geshe Sonam. *The Heart Sutra*. Translated by Ruth Sonam. Snow Lion Publications. Ithaca, NY. 2004. Pp. 69, 71, 79, 80.

The Healers Journal. "How to Use Sacred Mantras to Harmonize Brain Function and Balance the Chakras." July 16, 2013. www.thehealersjournal.com/2013/07/16/sacred-mantras-harmonize-brain-function-balance-chakras.

Toohill, Kathleen. "What Negative Thinking Does to Your Brain." Attn.com. July 31, 2015. www.attn.com/stories/2587/what-negative-thinking-does-your-brain.

Vitale, Dr. Joe. "I Love You, I'm Sorry, Forgive Me, Thank You. Ho'oponopono." WantToKnow.Info. As quoted by Dr. Ihaleakala Hew Len. www.wanttoknow.info/070701imsorryiloveyoujoevitale.

Williams, Ray. "Why New Year's Resolutions Fail." *Psychology Today*. December 27, 2010. www.psychologytoday.com/blog/wired-success/201012/why-new-years-resolutions-fail.

WEBSITE RESOURCES

About.com. "The Gayatri Mantra." http://hinduism.about.com/od/prayersmantras/a/The-Gayatri-Mantra.htm

Bhakti Breakfast Club. "Hey Ma Durga." www.bhaktibreakfastclub.com/mantraglossary44

Healthandyoga.com. "Mantras for You." www.healthandyoga.com/html/news/contentpage.aspx?book=rootfolder&page=mantra1

Humanity Healing University. "Om Gam Ganapataye Namaha." http://humanityhealing.net/2012/01/om-gam-ganapataye-namaha/

Kaur, Shakta. HariSingh.com. Video clip by Dr. Robert Svoboda. www.harisingh.com/ScienceOfMantra.htm

Motherhouse of the Goddess. "Om Mani Padme Hum." Translation. http://themotherhouseofthegoddess.com/2014/11/03/mantra-monday-om-mani-padme-hum-heart-chakra-work-with-the-goddess-kuan-yin

Project Happiness. "Science of Happiness." https://projecthappiness.com/the-science-of-happiness

StatisticBrain.com. "New Years Resolution Statistics." www.statisticbrain.com/new-years-resolution-statistics

SanskritMantra.com. "Some Simple Mantras for Those Just Starting Out," specifically: Om Sri Rama Jaya Rama, Jaya, Jaya Rama. www.sanskritmantra.com/article_info.php/some-simple-mantras-for-those-just-starting-out-a-12

The Chopra Center. "Using Shakti Mantras to Enhance Your Primordial Sound Mantra Practice." June 2013 Newsletter. www.chopra.com/teacher/jun13/vedic

The Energy Healing Site. "Chakra Tones." www.the-energy-healing-site.com/chakra-tones.html

Thittila, the Late Venerable Ashin. "Buddhist Metta."

www.abuddhistlibrary.com/Buddhism/B%20-%20Theravada/
Teachers/Sayadaw%20U.%20Thittilla/Buddhist%20Metta/
Buddhist%20Metta.htm

Wildmind Buddhist Meditation. "Definition of Mantra Meditation."
www.wildmind.org/mantras/definition

RESOURCES FOR MALA BEADS

Gillian Hurrie.
www.gillianhurrie.com/store/c1/Featured_Products.html

RESOURCES FOR SPIRITUAL MUSIC (FOUND ON ITUNES)

Alicia Mathewson. *Wise Innocence* album. AliciaMathewson.com.

Deva Premal: "Aham Prema."

Krishna Das.

Mirabai Ceiba: "Har Mukanday."

Snatam Kaur has a beautiful version of "Sa Ta Na Ma."

INDEX